C000181783

Town Walks

in

Cornwall

James Clancy

and

Simone Stanbrook–Byrne

CULM VALLEY PUBLISHING

Published by

Culm Valley Publishing Ltd
Culmcott House
Mill Street, Uffculme
Cullompton, Devon
EX15 3AT, UK
Tel: +44(0)1884 849085 Fax: +44(0)1884 840251
E-mail: info@culmvalleypublishing.co.uk
Website: www.culmvalleypublishing.co.uk

Copyright © Simone Stanbrook-Byrne & James Clancy. All photographs © James Clancy
The right of Simone Stanbrook-Byrne & James Clancy to be identified as Authors of this
Work has been asserted by them in accordance with the Copyright, Designs and Patents
Act 1988.

All rights reserved; no part of this publication may be reproduced, stored in a retrieval
system, or transmitted in any form or by any means, electronic, mechanical,
photocopying, recording or otherwise without the prior permission of the Publishers or a
license permitting copying in the UK issued by the Copyright Licensing Agency Ltd,
Saffron House, 6–10 Kirby Street, London EC1N 8TS.

While every effort has been made to ensure the accuracy of the information contained in
this book, the publisher and authors accepts no liability for incorrect information
regarding public footpaths and rights of way. Neither Culm Valley Publishing Ltd nor the
authors shall be liable for any damages whatsoever arising in any way from the use of or
inability to use this book, or any material contained within it, or from any action or
decision taken as a result of using this book. Follow the country code.

First published 2012

ISBN 978-1-907942-06-8 paperback

British Library Cataloguing-in-Publication Data
A catalogue record for this book is available from the British Library

Typeset by Culm Valley Publishing Ltd
Printed and bound by T.J. International Ltd, Padstow, Cornwall

Front cover image: The Quay, Padstow
Back cover image: Bull Hill, Fowey
All images used in this book are available as cards and prints from Culm Valley Publishing

Contents

Introduction   4

Disclaimer   5

Walk Locations   7

Walk 1 **St. Ives (2.25 miles)**   9

Walk 2 **Bude (3.25 miles)**   17

Walk 3 **Falmouth (1.75 miles)**   23

Walk 4 **Launceston (1 mile)**   29

Walk 5 **Liskeard (1.25 miles)**   37

Walk 6 **Looe (2.75 miles)**   45

Walk 7 **Lostwithiel (1 mile)**   53

Walk 8 **Marazion (1.8 miles)**   59

Walk 9 **Padstow (1.75 miles)**   65

Walk 10 **Wadebridge (2.75 miles)**   71

Walk 11 **Newquay (4.3 miles)**   78

Walk 12 **Truro (1.6 miles)**   87

Walk 13 **Penzance (2 miles)**   94

Walk 14 **Fowey (1.8 miles)**   101

Walk 15 **Helston (1.25 miles)**   108

Further Reading   116

Introduction

Throughout this book the directions for the walks are in black type enabling them to be picked out easily.

The history notes are in green italics. Of necessity, the history snippets are brief, designed to whet the appetite and encourage more research if you so desire.

Although we often start the walks from car parks, public transport access is given for each route.

Our sketch maps are not to scale. Used in conjunction with the text you should end up back where you started.

On any walk in town or country common sense must prevail: be properly shod, take care where you put your feet and be prepared for the weather. Although these walks are in towns and therefore close to amenities, it may be an idea to take food and first aid supplies plus a mobile phone.

We have thoroughly enjoyed preparing these routes – we hope you enjoy following them.

Antique Ted encountered on a walk

Disclaimer

Points that should be borne in mind:

Landmarks and buildings can change: buildings are demolished, new ones appear, road junctions change etc. In such cases a modicum of common sense must be exercised to keep yourself on the route, but we are always pleased to be advised of such changes.

Pavements and roads are usually well-maintained but please watch your step, accidents happen easily.

Watch out for traffic – please don't get mown down whilst stepping back to admire a building.

We hope that you enjoy these walks without mishap, but urge you to exercise caution at all times. Neither the authors nor Culm Valley Publishing Ltd accept responsibility for any misadventure which may occur during or arise from these walks and suggested routes.

Acknowledgements
Our grateful thanks to:

Alison Jeffery, Launceston VIC
Lynn Goold, The Ticket Shop & TIC, Fowey
John Buckingham, Padstow Museum
Linda Dutton, Padstow TIC
Mark Hibbard and Penny Carrington, Bude TIC
Mike Habbeshaw, Liskeard TIC
Mark Camp, Looe TIC
Sheila Harper, Newquay Old Cornwall Society
Nic, Ella and William Clancy
Tony Byrne

Towards Fowey town centre

Newquay Harbour

Walk Locations

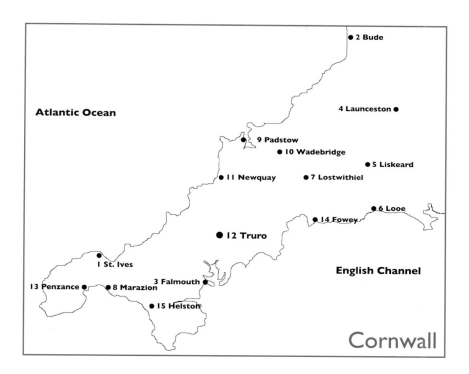

Walk 1	**St. Ives**		*Walk 11*	**Newquay**
Walk 2	**Bude**		*Walk 12*	**Truro**
Walk 3	**Falmouth**		*Walk 13*	**Penzance**
Walk 4	**Launceston**		*Walk 14*	**Fowey**
Walk 5	**Liskeard**		*Walk 15*	**Helston**
Walk 6	**Looe**			
Walk 7	**Lostwithiel**			
Walk 8	**Marazion**			
Walk 9	**Padstow**			
Walk 10	**Wadebridge**			

Walk 1

St Ives

Distance: 2¼ miles / 3.6km

St. Ives, renowned for its beautiful light, is world-famous as the haunt of artists and surfers. This is a walk of galleries, lovely restaurants, quaint cottages, and superb views – there aren't many town walks which can boast regular seal-sightings. You may even be treated to something larger as St. Ives made international news in 2007 when a great white shark was allegedly sighted off the coast here. Other similar reports appear from time to time. The mournful cry of gulls accompanies you throughout the walk, and you may find yourself amongst delightful, scurrying turnstones around the harbour. St. Ives is full of interesting backwaters with lots of nooks and crannies to peep into. There are a few ascents but the route is on good paths throughout – although one optional stretch involves a grassy path.

Start point: Outside Tate St. Ives, Porthmeor Beach, TR26 1TG

Directions to start: St. Ives is situated on the north coast in west Cornwall. It is 9 miles north of Penzance and can be accessed from the A30 at St. Erth

Parking: Various options including Porthmeor Car Park, TR26 1JU or Barnoon Car Park, Alexandra Rd, TR26 1JD

Public transport: St. Ives is well served by buses from: Camborne, Redruth, Truro, Penzance, St. Just, Newquay etc. Bus operators include First in Devon & Cornwall and Western Greyhound. Timetables available online at www.travelinesw.com. St. Ives railway station is located at Station Road, Trelyon Ave, TR26 2BP

Refreshments: The Cornish Deli, 3 Chapel St, 01736 795100; Porthgwidden Beach Café (all year), 01736 796791; Porthmeor Beach Café (Apr–Oct), 01736 793366

Toilets: Smeatons Pier, Porthgwidden Beach and The Lifeboat Station

Nearby places to stay: The Anchorage B&B, 5 Bunker's Hill, 07977 928540; Eleven Sea View Terrace, 01736 798440; Glanmor Guest House, The Belyars, 01736 795613; Little Leaf Guest House, 16 Park Ave, 01736 795427

Places of interest: Barbara Hepworth Museum and Sculpture Garden, Barnoon Hill, 01736 796226; St. Ives Museum, Wheal Dream, 01736 796005; Tate St. Ives, Porthmeor Beach, 01736 796226

Market days: St. Ives Farmers' Market takes place at The Guildhall,

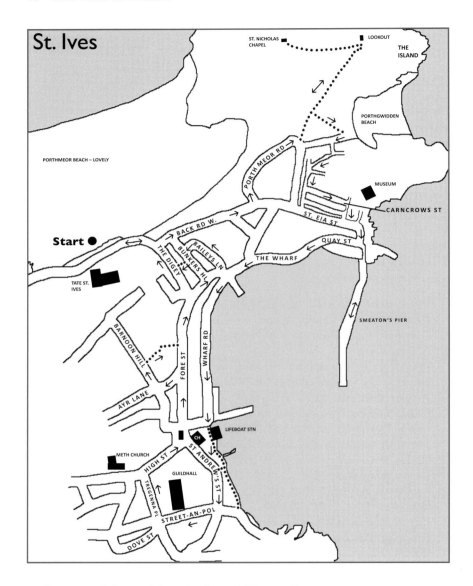

Street-an-Pol every Thursday from 9:30am to 2pm

Authors' tip: Seals are plentiful in the waters around St. Ives. Several boat companies offer trips to Seal Island, a favoured haunt of these popular marine mammals

Facing the beautiful Porthmeor Beach turn right away from the modern Tate St. Ives, a branch of the London gallery which opened in 1993. The road quickly bends right to past Digey Flats on the right, then left passing Harry's Court on the left. Notice the memorial on the wall of the cottage where artist Alfred Wallis lived. Pass Porthmeor Square and then an old church over to the right, now housing the St. Ives Society of Artists. Follow this road, Back Road West, passing the Bible Christian Chapel, then 30m further go left on Porthmeor Road.

The former church, which now is home to the **St. Ives Society of Artists,** *was built at the beginning of the 20thC and dedicated to St. Nicholas, patron saint of fishermen and seafarers. Originally an Anglican church, many of the residents of the town were Methodists and by the 1940s the church had fallen into disrepair. During WWII it was requisitioned as a field hospital and was taken over by the Society of Artists in 1945*

The Bible Christian Chapel *is one of the many non-conformist churches which you will see throughout St. Ives. Historically, the residents were reputedly rather disenchanted with the Anglican Church because of tithes levied on the fishing industry. John Wesley preached here on many occasions and his influence was strong in the town. This little chapel was bought by the Bible Christians in 1858 from the Wesleyans who built it in 1824*

Porthmeor Beach with The Island beyond

This winds around a bit, follow it as far as The Island Car Park on the left. Enter here, minding out for cars, and pick up the tarmac path beyond the car park which goes up to the battery on the headland. Away to your right is Godrevy Lighthouse and up to your left is the delightful chapel of St. Nicholas. On the headland you find a National Coastwatch Institution Station. If you wish to visit the chapel it's a pleasant grassy stroll, after which return to the car park.

> **The Island** was originally a fort, the old name for it being 'Pendinas' which means 'fortified headland'. There was once a battery on The Island which was armed during the Napoleonic Wars. The modern National Coastwatch Institution lookout here enjoys superb views with frequent sightings of passing marine mammals. The delightful little **Chapel of St. Nicholas** on its exposed hill has been there since 'time immemorial' and a chapel has certainly stood here since at least the 14th or 15thC. The building narrowly missed being completely demolished in the early 20thC and was restored in 1911 to commemorate the coronation of George V. It is Grade II listed

When you arrive back at the car park bear diagonally left across it to the far corner. Here you will find two descending flights of steps. Take the one which goes towards the beach. These steps lead to the road beside the Porthgwidden Beach Café. You now reach a section of the walk with lots of little turnings in quick succession. Turn right by the beach café, away from the sea, and uphill to

The Island

Houses near the Quay

another road with public loos on the corner. Turn left. In another 20m you meet a T-junction where you go right, away from the sea and past attractive cottages. At the next T-junction go left and then keep ahead for a short distance until you find Carncrows Street on the left. Turn along here and at the end turn right into Carncrows Road passing Teetotal Street on the right.

At the end of Carncrows Road at the T-junction go left along St. Eia Street. You quickly reach another T-junction at Sea View Place. To the left is St. Ives Museum but the walk turns right and you swiftly reach another junction at which you keep ahead along the now narrow, cobbled road. This leads to another T-junction with Smeaton's Pier to the left. Walk along the pier, past the little dumpy lantern tower to the only-slightly taller lighthouse at the end. From the end of the pier you have a good view across to Porthminster Beach and the headlands along the coast. Look out for the plaque near the end lighthouse commemorating the engineers who constructed the pier.

__Smeaton's Pier__ was built in the 18thC and extended in the 19thC by about 100m, to include the further lighthouse. The pier's designer, John Smeaton, is more famous for creating the third Eddystone Lighthouse. This Grade II* listed pier was built by Thomas Richardson who had been Smeaton's mason on the Eddystone Lighthouse

---

*The mediæval **St. Leonard's Chapel** provided a place for fishermen to pray before setting out on frequently perilous journeys. It is Grade II listed and was renovated in the 1970s*

Retrace your steps along the pier to the mainland, looking out for the diminutive St. Leonard's Chapel, attached to the back of the gents' loos on the left. Turn left at the end of the pier and keep ahead along the cobbled Quay Street which runs into The Wharf. The harbour is to your left with shops, galleries and restaurants on the right. Keep ahead, passing the 14thC Sloop Inn and Fish Street on the right, then the back of Fore Street Methodist Church. The tower of the parish church peeps over the roofs to your right. Continue ahead on the path between

St. Ia's Church

St. Ives Lifeboat Station and the high wall surrounding the church. After the end of the church wall (where there is a nice view through to the church) keep on a little further and then take the next path on the right, away from the sea. In about 15m you reach St. Andrew's Street, turn left.

At a small, staggered crossroads you will see the St. Ives Art Club to the left but you turn right. This is Street-An-Pol which leads you past the rather grand Guildhall, built in 1938, on the right. At the top of the road turn right, passing the library building on the left. At the end of the road look left to see the magnificent United Methodist Community Church, completed in 1898, then turn right along the High Street towards the parish church.

> **Parish Church:** *Legend has it that St. Ia was an Irish princess of the 5th or 6thC who was martyred on the River Hayle and buried on the site of this church which is dedicated to her. The town derives its name from her. The present church, with its 80-foot tower, dates from the first half of the 15thC although earlier churches would have occupied the site*

> **A Market House** *has stood here since the end of the 15thC although the present building dates from 1832 and is Grade II listed. It was built at a cost of £840. The original Town Hall occupied the first floor where there were also cells for prisoners. It was one of the first public buildings in the town to receive gas lighting in the mid 19thC*

When you reach St. Ia's Church, with the old Market House on the left, go left to pass between the church and the market. Beyond here, cross the road and walk straight ahead along Fore Street. You'll pass one of our favourites along here – the friendly St. Ives Bookseller, a really good independent bookshop rubbing shoulders with many other interesting shops. About 60m along Fore Street you reach a sharp left bend, go up here to another tiny, staggered crossroads with the entrance to the Barbara Hepworth Museum opposite.

> **Barbara Hepworth** *was born in Yorkshire in 1910. Her sculptures are displayed all over the world, including the United Nations Building in New York, but it is at her home and garden here in St. Ives, to which she moved in 1949, that the largest collection of her wonderful work can be found. The garden is even beautiful when it's raining. She died in a fire at this studio in 1975. The studio has been part of Tate since 1980*

Turn right along Barnoon Hill, taking the steps up its right hand side. At the top turn right down Barnoon Terrace and keep heading down the narrow path between walls. Beside No. I Academy Cottage you will find descending steps. Go down here to land once again in Fore Street for further browsing.

Turn left, passing the intriguingly named Court Cocking on the right (probably named after the small fishing boats called 'cockyns') and Salubrious Place on the left. You will also pass the Primitive Methodist Church of 1831 on the right, then Bunkers Hill and Bailey's Lane on the left. Go up the cobbled Bailey's Lane. At the top glance back to get a good view of the lighthouse, then turn left (a sign on the wall here helpfully tells you you're in Norway) and immediately left again, then go right up some steps.

The path levels out then descends a few further steps. At the bottom go right, through a roofed passageway, to emerge onto The Digey. Glance opposite here along Hicks Court with its lovely stone arch, remnant of the house which belonged to George Hicks, a town official of the 17thC. Turn right along The Digey. At the end of its cobbles continue ahead – you now retrace your steps past Digey Flats and round to Porthmeor Beach and Tate St. Ives where you started.

The Digey

Bude

Distance: 3¼ miles / 5.2 km

Bude is very close to the Devon border with Cornwall and has the feel of both counties. It has been a popular seaside resort since Victorian times when the railway was extended to Bude to bring holidaymakers (ironically there is now no railway here). It has some lovely historic areas and the stretch of the walk alongside the rejuvenated canal (originally built 1819–26) is appealing. This is a walk of open spaces. The route is fairly level, slightly rough underfoot along Church Lane and with lots of options for refreshment.

Start point: The Crescent Car Park, Bencoolen Rd, EX23 8LE

Directions to start: Bude is on the north Cornwall coast, 18 miles north west of Launceston. It is easily accessed off the A39

Parking: The Crescent Car Park, Bencoolen Rd, EX23 8LE

Public transport: Bude is well served by buses from: Plymouth, Saltash, Callington, Launceston, Bideford, Barnstaple, Holsworthy, Boscastle, Okehampton, Exeter etc. Bus operators include First in Devon & Cornwall, Stagecoach Devon and Western Greyhound. Timetables available online at www.travelinesw.com. Nearest railway station is Okehampton, Devon (24.8 miles)

Refreshments: G's Café and Diner, 15 Queen St, 01288 353160; Life's a Beach, Summerleaze Beach, 01288 355222

Toilets: In the car park

Nearby places to stay: Breakwater House, 3 Breakwater Rd, 01288 353137; Falcon Hotel, Breakwater Rd, 01288 352005; Fairway House Guest House, 8 Downs View, 01288 355059

Places of interest: Bude Castle Heritage Centre, The Wharf, 01288 357300; Tourist Information and Canal Visitor Centre, The Crescent Car Park, 01288 354240

Market days: Bude Farmers' Market, held on the Wharf by the canal runs every Friday from 10am–3pm from April–September

Authors' tip: Tintagel and Boscastle are not far away along the coast and are both well worth visiting for their history and stunning locations

From the car park turn left along Bencoolen Road towards the bridge, opposite which you see the Falcon Hotel. Immediately after the bridge turn right to walk along Breakwater Road beside the canal with a sea view ahead. Pass Breakwater House and as you proceed you see, beyond the canal on your right, the River

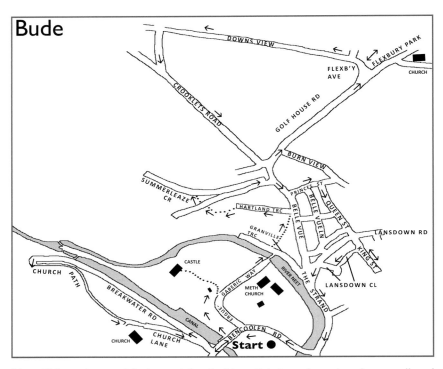

Neet. When the road forks go left, climbing slightly and passing the castellated Penrock House. As the road bends left back on itself keep with it passing Efford Cottage on the right. Follow this unmade road, with its attractive houses. This is Church Path which becomes Church Lane.

The Falcon *derives its name from the bird on the crest of the Acland family, local landowners and patrons of The Falcon during its early years. It has been one of Bude's watering holes for over two centuries, starting life in 1798 when it was a lodging house for sea captains whose ships were moored in Bude Haven. It was extended after the opening of the canal. Alfred, Lord Tennyson stayed here and broke a leg when he fell over the garden wall. Bude is mentioned in Tennyson's poem Guinevere*

Efford Cottage: *Once a storage 'cellar' for ships' cargoes it was converted to a holiday cottage by the Aclands who stayed here in the 19thC*

You reach the Church of St. Michael and All Angels. This is worth a visit with its lofty and imposing interior. The walk continues on Church Lane back to The

Falcon Hotel. Re-cross the bridge, noticing the old lifeboat house over on the right opposite the hotel. This was built in the first half of the 19thC and is now a holiday cottage. Immediately after the bridge go left to walk beside the water, a lovely spot with accompanying birdlife. After about 100m you reach a car park area, bear right between the library and community fire station towards a tall pinnacle – the Bude Light

The Church of St. Michael and All Angels *was built in 1834, a gift to the town from Thomas Dyke Acland. It is Grade II listed. Its organ dates from 1923 and the font is housed in its own little side chapel. The church was originally a 'chapel of ease' with the main church being at Stratton, but later this became the parish church*

Bude Castle *was built in 1830 as the home of Cornish inventor Goldsworthy Gurney who was born near Padstow in 1793. He qualified in medicine by the age of 20 but was also very accomplished in the fields of chemistry and mechanics and carried out work with steam engines. Goldsworthy Gurney invented the 'Bude Light' – an oil and oxygen system which produced very bright light and was used to light the House of Commons. His achievements in this area earned him a knighthood in 1863. A single Bude Light lit his castle, utilising prisms and lenses to distribute the light around the house. The building itself was constructed on a 'raft' of concrete on the sand, another of its owner's*

Bude Castle

designs. He died in straightened circumstances in 1875.The modern-day **Bude Light** *pinnacle was designed by Cornish concrete sculptor Carole Vincent. It utilises fibre-optics to light it at night. It was constructed as a millennium project and, around its base, depicts the night sky as seen on 17 May 2000*

From here you have a good view of Bude Castle – visit it and then return to the road leading away from the Bude Light towards the complex of Methodist Church buildings about 100m away. Keep along Ergue-Gaberic Way passing the church on your right with the rising ground of Shalder Hill behind it. The road leads to an attractive, brightly painted footbridge across the river. Cross this and ascend steps, bearing left at the top to turn right in about 20m at the end of Granville Terrace. Look left as you ascend to see the climbing wall on the back of an adventure centre. At the top of the road you reach the shopping street of Belle Vue. Go left and immediately left again along Hartland Terrace.

Shalder Hill *is a sand dune which has become isolated from the coast due to the development of adjacent land. It is a prime site for botanists and the war memorial and a meteorological station are sited on it. Before the installation of the automated weather station a local man, Harvey Kendall, Bude's meteorological officer since 1971, climbed the hill every day to take readings*

Inside St. Michael and All Angels   *Bude Light*

Crossing the River Neet

Pass the Hartland Hotel on the right and keep ahead on the footpath, you are heading towards the coast and Summerleaze Beach. The path bends, follow it and cross the road to continue on the path beyond towards a terrace of tall town houses. When you reach them pause to look around, the views are good. Turn right, with the houses to your left, and walk along Summerleaze Crescent. At the end turn left, again on Belle Vue. The road forks in about 30m, take the right option here to walk across the golf course which is not as dodgy as it sounds – the course is fenced from the road and pedestrians. Ahead to the left, in the far distance, you can see a GCHQ satellite station on the hills. Directly ahead and closer to hand you see the impressive sight of another Methodist Church, aim for this. When you reach the end of the golf course keep ahead along Flexbury Park to the church. At the time of writing its future was in doubt.

Flexbury Methodist Church *is Grade II listed and was built in 1905, some of its timbers coming from a cargo ship which foundered in a storm. Recently the foundations have been undermined and the church has closed*

From the church return along Flexbury Park and before the golf course turn right along Flexbury Avenue to skirt the links. This road becomes Downs View. When you reach Ocean View Road on the right turn left to re-cross the golf course, there is no pavement here. At the next junction turn left back towards town.

Flexbury Methodist Church   *King Street*

Once you reach the town keep straight ahead along Belle Vue (again!) and in 100m go left down Princes Street. In another 70m turn right along Queen Street and at the end of Queen Street cross Lansdown Road, then keep straight ahead along King Street. This is a short and pretty road. Stroll to its end and then come back down to take the narrow Lansdown Close which leads off it. This opens up into a small car park. The police station is beyond on the left, turn right and the road leads you back to Lansdown Road.

> **King Street** *is a conservation area. Many of its houses are owned by the Blanchminster Trust which originated as the Blanchminster Charity in 1421 and is possibly the oldest charitable trust in Britain. It provides educational and other assistance for local people*

Here you will find an attractive public garden ahead of you, turn left, passing the Barclays Bank building on the left with its rather notable clock. Follow the main road as it bears left, over to your right now you have good views of the complex of buildings around the Methodist Church which you passed earlier in the walk. Some of these buildings are now in use as a doctors' surgery and the Citizen's Advice Bureau. Continue along the pavement beside the river, this is The Strand and you are approaching a road bridge ahead. Turn right to cross the bridge and your start point is a few metres along on the left.

Walk 3
Falmouth
Distance: 1¾ miles / 2.8km

Falmouth is an attractive coastal town with a genteel air about it. It received its charter to hold a market in the mid 17thC and it was at Falmouth that news of Nelson's death during the Battle of Trafalgar in 1805 first reached England. Some ascent and descent is encountered during the walk but nothing too onerous, the paths are good throughout and the cry of the gulls keeps you going. Falmouth boasts some really excellent places to eat.

Start point: National Maritime Museum Car Park, Avenue Rd, TR11 4BS

Directions to start: Falmouth is located on the River Fal on the south coast of Cornwall approximately 11½ south west of Truro. The A39 runs into the town

Parking: National Maritime Museum Car Park, Avenue Rd, TR11 4BS

Public transport: Falmouth is well served by buses from: Penzance, Helston, Truro, Camborne, Redruth, Penryn, Newquay etc. Bus operators include First in Devon & Cornwall, OTS and Western Greyhound. Timetables available online at www.travelinesw.com. Falmouth Railway Station is on Avenue Rd, TR11 4AZ

Refreshments: De Wynns, 55 Church St, 01326 319259; Dolly's Tea Room and Wine Bar, 21 Church St, 01326 218400; Harbour View Café, 24 Arwenack St, 01326 315315

Toilets: Near car park and museum area on Arwenack Street

Nearby places to stay: Bosanneth Guest House, Gyllyngvase Hill, 01326 314 649; The Falmouth Town House, 3 Grove Place, 01326 312009; Highcliffe Contemporary B&B, 22 Melvill Rd, 01326 314466

Places of interest: Falmouth Art Gallery, Municipal Building, The Moor, 01326 313863; National Maritime Museum Cornwall, Discovery Quay 01326 313388; Pendennis Castle, Castle Close, 01326 316594; Trebah Garden, Mawnan Smith, 01326 252200

Market days: Farmers' Market every Tuesday at The Moor, 9am–2pm

Authors' tip: We recommend taking the 20-minute trip on a ferry over to St. Mawes to explore this large picturesque village and its castle

From the car park walk out onto the main road, Arwenack Street, noticing the big spike of the Killigrew Monument to the right of the car park. Opposite you is lovely Arwenack House. Turn left along the road, away from the town centre,

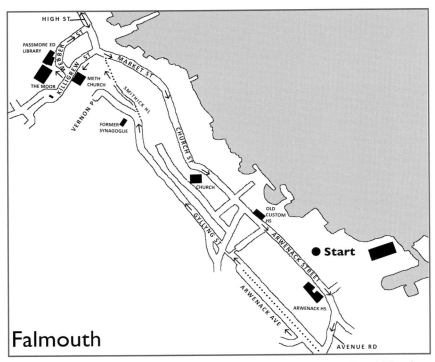

Falmouth

and very soon, at the mini roundabout, turn right on Avenue Road. The first turning on the right along here is Arwenack Avenue. Take this, following the central path between the lichen-encrusted trees through this attractive residential area.

Commemorating the eminent local family, the **Killigrew Monument** was built in 1737 by Martin Killigrew who owned Arwenack House at that time

Arwenack House, the oldest domestic building in Falmouth, was originally owned by the Arwenack family and the oldest part of the house dates back to the 14thC, although little of this remains. Succeeding centuries have seen much alteration, particularly after damage during the Civil War. The Killigrews lived here from the end of the 14thC

At the end of the path continue ahead, passing the early 19thC School of Art on the left, to go through the impressive, ball-topped, stone gateposts, originally the entrance to the Arwenack estate. Beyond these cross the road and continue ahead up Gyllyng Street. You pass Gyllyng Hall on the right, now converted for residential use. Keep going, enjoying lovely views to the right over the town and across the estuary towards the village of Flushing on the other side.

The School of Art *was built at the beginning of the 20thC in memory of Anna Maria Fox, a member of the Quaker family which did much for Falmouth during the 19thC including conception of the idea for the* **Royal Cornwall Polytechnic Society** *(later in walk). Anna's wish for a facility where engineering models created by workers at the nearby Perran Foundry, which her family ran, could be put on show, resulted in the Society's foundation in 1832. It developed as a charity promoting education, culture and science and received royal patronage in 1835. Anna died in 1897*

The road begins to descend and you will see a small public garden up to the left. Keep ahead and you reach an area of car parking. Beyond this the road forks, go left to pass the former Falmouth Synagogue. Just beyond here take the steps down to the right and at the bottom turn left, passing the Old Bakehouse of 1835 on the left. This is Smithick Hill.

Falmouth Synagogue *is a Grade II listed building and was in use for its intended purpose from 1808–1880 after which the local Jewish population diminished. An earlier synagogue had been sited at Fish Strand Quay. The building was later used as a furniture store and is now a private dwelling*

Arwenack House

At the end of Smithick Hill, beside a house called Boswynn, follow the footpath downhill – a railing is there to aid your descent if you need it. At the bottom go left along Market Street and at the junction go left again onto Killigrew Street. This opens up into a broad area known as The Moor with some glorious buildings. The mighty Methodist Church is on your left with the steep steps of Jacob's Ladder beyond it, built by a local businessman to provide access between some of his various properties. Keep ahead to the memorial in the middle of the road and here cross over towards the decorative fountain which was moved to its present location from the old market.

The Methodist Church *was built in 1874 to replace an earlier church on the same site. It was severely bombed during WWII and was restored and reopened in 1956*

Memorial: *This was built in 1898 in memory of the officers and men of HM Post Office and Packet Services which carried overseas mail from Falmouth from 1688–1850*

Turn right and walk back along the other side of The Moor/Killigrew Street, passing the former post office on the left with its decorative clock and ironwork and the 1894 Passmore Edwards Library (see note in Truro walk). Keep ahead after this along Webber Street passing the imposing 18thC building on the left

The Passmore Edwards Library

High Street

which now houses the Women's Institute. At the T-junction go left up High Street. This is a 'there-and-back-again' section to savour the delightful buildings up here, including the old Town Hall which now houses an antique shop. Remember to peep down the attractive nooks and crannies which lead off this main road, including Barrack's Ope just before you reach the arch straddling the road.

> **The Old Town Hall** *was originally a chapel and possibly dates from the beginning of the 18thC. It has served as a gaol, council offices and a courthouse. It was here that, in the late 19thC, the trial of shipwrecked sailors accused of cannibalism commenced before transferring to Exeter*

> **Barrack's Ope:** *Opes are covered alleyways between buildings providing access to the waterfront or residential areas*

Return down the High Street and keep ahead on Market Street, an appealing shopping precinct with modern shops in delightful old buildings. Watch out for traffic – it isn't pedestrianised although it feels like it is. Pass St. George's Arcade on the right – opposite it is the lovely De Wynn's 19thC coffee shop.

> **St. George's Arcade** *originally opened as a cinema in 1912, when it was one of the largest in the country. It was damaged during WWII and converted to shops in the 1960s*

The Church of King Charles the Martyr, *one of only seven churches in England with this dedication, was built in the 1660s and enlarged in later years. It is Grade II* listed and has many beautiful features including a graceful, wrought iron screen*

Keep ahead, the road becomes Church Street, you pass another of our well-liked independent bookshops on the right and the 1835 Royal Cornwall Polytechnic Society. You reach the church, which is well worth a visit, then keep along the road as it bends and becomes Arwenack Street. Look out for the old Custom House on the left. Keep going, passing elegant town houses on the right, until you find yourself back at the Killigrew Monument and the car park

---

The Custom House *is another Grade II* building dating from 1814, although a Custom House has existed in the town on different sites since 1650. Several other custom houses were built in this Greek-revival style*

King Charles the Martyr

Walk 4

Launceston

Distance: 1 mile / 1.6km

Named for a former monastery dedicated to St. Stephen (Lannstefan) which was situated outside the present town, Launceston is steeped in history. It was once the site of a Royal Mint and was the only walled town in Cornwall. John Couch Adams, the astronomer who discovered the planet Neptune, was born on a farm just outside the town in 1819. Launceston is dominated by the ruins of the Norman castle and has many other historic sites. This short, easy walk encompasses ancient gatehouses, an ornate church, quaint shopping streets and far-reaching country views. The route is on good paths throughout with no strenuous uphill sections although there are a few steps. Tea shops abound.

Start point: Walk House Car Park, Tower St, PL15 8BQ

Directions to start: Launceston is situated in east Cornwall close to the Devon border. It lies equidistant between the towns of Okehampton and Bodmin and is easily accessible from the A30

Parking: Walk House Car Park, Tower St, (max 3 hours)

Public transport: Launceston is well served by buses from: Plymouth, Bude, Tavistock, Liskeard, Exeter, Newquay, Bodmin etc. Bus operators include First in Devon & Cornwall, Group Travel and Western Greyhound. Timetables available online at www.travelinesw.com. Nearest railway stations are Gunnislake (10.4 miles) and Calstock (11.7 miles)

Refreshments: Jericho's Brasserie, 4 Northgate St, 01566 770080; The Mad Hatters, 28 Church St, 01566 774634; No 8, 8 Westgate St, 01566 777369

Toilets: Walk House Car Park and Race Hill Car Park

Nearby places to stay: Beechgrove B&B, 47a Dunheved Rd, 01566 779455; Eagle House Hotel, 3 Castle St, 01566 774488

Places of interest: Lawrence House Museum, Castle St, 01566 773277; Tamar Otters & Wildlife Centre, North Petherwin, 01566 785646; Launceston Steam Railway, St. Thomas Rd, 01566 775665

Market days: Launceston Butter Market runs in the Town Square from March to December on every 1st and 3rd Saturday. This general market also features on Tuesdays during the months of August and December

Authors' tip: Just north of town the Launceston Steam Railway is a nearby and worthwhile excursion. This narrow gauge system offers a 5-mile round trip through the attractive Kensey Valley

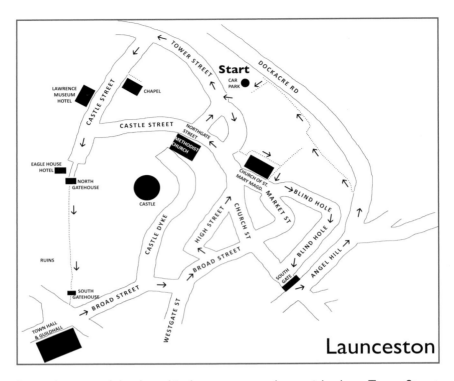

Launceston

Leave the car park by the vehicular entrance and turn right down Tower Street. After 100m take the first left along Castle Street. A few metres along here on the left you will see steps leading up to the attractive-looking Northgate Street. Enjoy the view up it but continue to walk along Castle Street, passing on the left the 19thC, Grade II listed, Castle Street Chapel, formerly a Congregational chapel. This road is flanked by other attractive buildings including Lawrence House Museum. John Betjeman described Castle Street as having a "perfect collection of 18thC town houses". The road bends left opposite the Eagle House Hotel but the walk continues straight ahead between high walls with the rising ground of the castle to your left.

Lawrence House Museum *This lovely Grade II listed Georgian house, built in 1753, is owned by the National Trust and is now managed as a museum by the Town Council. It is open seasonally and is well worth a visit, housing portraits and a sculpture of astronomer John Couch Adams, amongst many other interesting exhibits*

Eagle House Hotel *is an elegant Georgian town house built in 1764 by the Constable of the Castle. Some of its stone comes from the partly demolished North Gatehouse of the castle. It has also served as a Town Hall*

Launceston Castle *was originally a typical 'motte and bailey' construction, which comprised a wooden keep on a mound or 'motte' surrounded by an enclosure or 'bailey'. This was built around 1067 and was known as Dunheved. The Castle became the seat of the Earls of Cornwall and in the 13thC Richard, a younger brother of Henry III, extensively rebuilt the castle in stone to include curtain walls, gatehouses, a round tower within the keep and a great hall, the layout of which can clearly be seen today. In 1337, Edward III created the Duchy of Cornwall and his eldest son, Edward the Black Prince, became Duke, carrying out more restoration on the castle, although it was subsequently neglected and fell into disrepair. During the Civil War the castle's defence walls were in such a state of decay that Cromwell's army didn't feel any need to damage them further on capturing the castle from the Royalists. By the mid 17thC the only habitable section of the castle was the North Gatehouse. The great hall was in use as an assize hall until the 17thC. Over the centuries this place has witnessed many hangings, the last execution taking place in 1821 at the prison which was sited at the castle until 1842. This was known as Dooms-*

St. Lawrence House Museum, Castle Street

Dale, having a reputation for filth and barbarity. In 1973 Prince Charles was invested as Duke of Cornwall at Launceston Castle

Keep ahead through the stone arch of North Gatehouse on the path towards South Gatehouse, with good views of the Norman castle ruins up to the left and further ruins of the mediæval buildings ahead of you to the right. There are also expansive country views further to the right. The path through this area is permitted by the Duchy of Cornwall and the Department of Culture, Media and Sport. Emerge through South Gatehouse, which in the Middle Ages led into the Earl of Cornwall's private deer park, looking out for the portcullis slot in the arch above you. Through the gate you will see the grand Town Hall and Guildhall. Turn left to follow the castle's curtain wall on your left and when the wall swings left again keep ahead towards the town centre.

The Town Hall and Guildhall *are adjacent Grade II listed buildings built in the rather striking Victorian Gothic style. The former dates from 1887 and the latter from 1881. They can be hired as grand venues for private functions*

Soon you reach the main shopping area with Broad Street and the market place to your left. Glance right down attractive Westgate Street but turn left to approach the prominent and attractive war memorial. Pass the memorial on your right hand side looking out for the engraved paving slab marking the site

S. Gatehouse, Town Hall & Guildhall beyond   St. Mary Magdalene's Church

Church Street

of the martyrdom of Cuthbert Mayne. Beyond the memorial leave the square along High Street with its lovely old buildings, the overhanging houses on the right date from 1555. Ahead of you the Church of St. Mary Magdalene will come into view. At the junction spare a glance back to the right along attractive Church Street then cross over to visit the church.

Cuthbert Mayne *was born in Barnstaple, N. Devon c. 1544 and educated at the grammar school. He became a Protestant minister at the age of 18, following in the footsteps of his uncle who was a Church of England priest. He subsequently studied at Oxford where he became chaplain and it was during his sojourn there that he met some influential Catholics, including Edmund Campion (ancestor of one of the authors). Cuthbert eventually converted. Elizabeth I did not take kindly to Catholics and in 1577 Cuthbert, who was by now residing in Cornwall, was arrested and imprisoned in Dooms-Dale. He refused to recognise the queen as head of the church and, like many Catholics, was regarded as a threat to her. He was hung drawn and quartered on 29 November 1577 and was canonised by Pope Paul VI in 1970. The town's Catholic Church is dedicated to him*

The Church of St. Mary Magdalene *dates from the early 16thC and is frequently regarded as being one of the finest churches in England. It is*

St. Mary Magdalene's Church with its carved granite walls

remarkable for its beautifully carved granite exterior walls. The mainly Victorian interior is rich with history, notice the elaborately carved pulpit and pew ends

Leave the church and turn right to continue ahead along Northgate Street, you will see the large Methodist Church to your left with the castle behind and above it. In a few metres, opposite the Methodist Church, take a right turn (this is the 2nd right after leaving St. Mary Magdalene) and soon go right again along an ancient-feeling stretch of Tower Street, passing the 17thC Bell Inn on your right.

You swiftly reach St. Mary Magdalene's again, look out for the narrow path on the left running round the church. Take this, walking round the building and admiring the splendid yew trees adorning the graveyard. The path leads round to a road along which you turn left, away from the church. The road soon forks at the market building, keep left to go down the road known as Blind Hole which soon bends right then narrows, the old buildings on the left being built on the former town wall. Blind Hole leads out to Southgate Street and the massive arch of South Gate.

The Grade I listed **South Gate** *is the only surviving example of three gateways into the old walled town. It dates back to the 14thC and would once have housed a portcullis. In the mid 15thC the princely sum of £3.8s.0112d (£3.40) was spent on smartening it up. The two rooms above the arch are mid*

16thC and in the 18thC it was a prison for petty offenders and debtors which, like Dooms-Dale, was renowned for its squalidness. In 1884 it ceased to function as such and became a museum until the mid 20thC when it commenced life as an antique shop and then an art gallery. Its battlements were constructed to commemorate the golden jubilee of Queen Victoria. In 2010 it was used as offices for the Town Council while the Town Hall underwent restoration

The walk goes left through the arch but first turn right and look up to your right to see the blue plaque marking the birthplace of Philip Gidley King.

South Gate

Philip Gidley King *was born in Launceston in 1758. He joined the Royal Navy at the age of 12 and rose to the position of Captain. He sailed to New South Wales with the aim of establishing a convict settlement there, then in 1788 set up a settlement on Norfolk Island. His first son, with female convict Ann Inett, eventually became the first Australian-born officer of the Royal Navy. Philip King and Ann Inett had two sons together but subsequently married other people. Philip King became Lieutenant Governor of Norfolk Island in 1791 and Governor of New South Wales in 1800. Ann Inett's crime had been the theft of 12 shillings-worth of clothing in Worcester. She had been sentenced to death, this being commuted to 7 years transportation. She eventually returned to England and died around 1825. Philip King died in England in 1808*

Go through the South Gate and turn left down Angel Hill with views of the open countryside ahead. At the bottom of Angel Hill go left and within 20m and opposite the back of an interesting old farmhouse take a cobbled pathway going left up off the road. Climb some steps and continue ahead at the top along a path which soon leads to a broad sandy area with wonderful views towards Devon and the tors of Dartmoor. There are several benches here which lend themselves as a nice picnic site if you're not partaking of Launceston's refuelling stops. The churchyard of St. Mary Magdalene is to the left. Walk across this area towards some old cottages in front of which you find a path. Turn right along it and descend steps. Turn left at the bottom to pass attractive houses, this path is known as The Walk. Keep on The Walk for about 60m until you find a gateway on the left leading to more steps. Go up here and at the top you find the car park from which you started.

Liskeard

Distance: 1¼ miles / 2km

Mentioned in the Domesday Book of 1086, Liskeard was first granted a charter to hold a market in 1240. From the 14thC it was one of the principal Cornish stannary towns and the prosperity which, in later centuries, resulted from silver, copper and lead mining gave birth to many of Liskeard's beautiful buildings in and around its attractive town centre. The walk has a few ascents and descents but is on good paths.

Start point: From the vehicular entrance of Westbourne Car Park, PL14 6BW

Directions to start: Liskeard is situated 20 miles west of Plymouth in south east Cornwall. It is easily accessible from both the A38 and the A390

Parking: Westbourne Car Park, West St, PL14 6BW

Public transport: Liskeard is well served by buses from: Launceston, Tavistock, Callington, Bodmin, St. Austell, Plymouth, Looe, St. Columb Major, Truro etc. Bus operators include First in Devon & Cornwall, Roselyn Coaches and Western Greyhound. Timetables available online at www.travelinesw.com. Liskeard Railway Station is located at Station Rd, PL14 4DX

Refreshments: Fat Frog, 6a Market St, 01579 348818; Liskeard Tavern, Liskeard Retail Park PL14 3PR, 01579 341752; The Old Stag, Station Rd, 01579 342280

Toilets: In the car park

Nearby places to stay: The Nebula Hotel, Higher Lux St, 01579 343989; Pencubitt Country House Hotel, Lamellion Cross, 01579 342694

Places of interest: Carnglaze Caverns, nr St. Neot, 01579 320251; Liskeard and District Museum, Foresters Hall, Pike St, 01579 346087; Stuart House Trust, Barras St, 01579 347347

Market days: WI market on Fridays in the Long Room at the Public Hall. The cattle market is on alternate Thursdays. Occasional street markets, particularly at Christmas and at St. Matthew's Fair in October

---

Authors' tip: Consider a train ride to the seaside town of Looe. The ride from Liskeard is very picturesque and gets increasingly scenic as you approach the coast via the riverside track

---

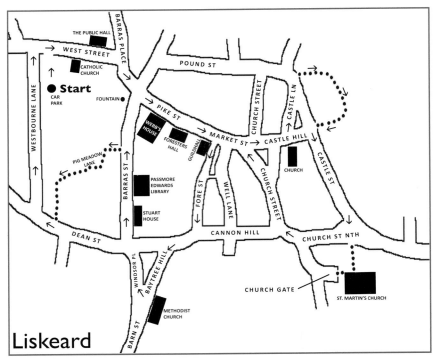

Liskeard

Leave the car park via the vehicular entrance and turn right along West Street, soon passing the 1866 Catholic Church on the right. There are some attractive buildings opposite, including the Public Hall. At the end of West Street go right along Barras Place and continue as it runs into The Parade, an open area with elegant buildings surrounding an ornamental fountain – look out for the Masonic Hall to the left of The White Horse pub. Cross the road junction to walk down Pike Street which runs beside Webb's House. You are heading towards the museum in Foresters Hall with the lovely clock tower on the Guildhall beyond.

The Public Hall was built in 1890 and houses the Town Council offices. It serves as a venue for a variety of community activities. The main hall seats 300 people

The Fountain: Former Mayor, Michael Loam, presented the ornamental drinking fountain on The Parade to Liskeard in 1871. This was in honour of his father (also Michael Loam), a Cornish engineer who, inspired by German designs, introduced the man engine (a revolutionary device for lifting men up and down deep mineshafts). Constructed from a series of moving platforms it *was used in many mines throughout Cornwall and west Devon from 1842 into the early 20thC*

The Masonic Hall *is not as old as it looks. It was designed in 1872 by architect John Paul. This Grade II listed building was constructed in a Ruskinian Venetian Gothic style*

Webb's House *formerly Webb's Hotel, is a grade II listed building dating from 1833. As an hotel it was frequently used as a meeting place for South Caradon Mine where the purser would present the accounts reflecting the copper mining successes. The building is currently home of The Cornish Times, a local newspaper that first saw publication in January 1857*

Foresters Hall *originally housed the East Cornwall Savings Bank when it was built in 1861 (the 1896 date inscribed on the building is misleading). Today it serves as a home for the Tourist Information Office and Liskeard & District Museum. This grade II listed building, with its Venetian Gothic-style stonework, was designed by the locally prolific architect Henry Rice, responsible for over 100 buildings in the town*

Pike Street becomes Market Street, continue ahead passing Well Lane on the right and beyond this there is a meeting of narrow ways. Bear slightly left and

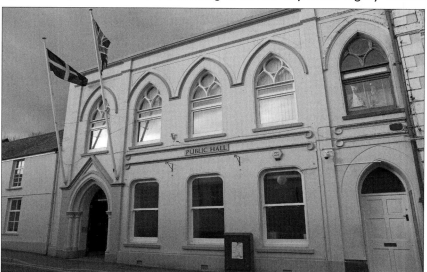

The Public Hall

then walk ahead up Castle Hill. This climbs to the Seventh Day Adventist Church on the right at which point turn left along Castle Lane.

The Guildhall *was built in 1859 replacing the former Town Hall. This grade II* listed building has seen use not only as a Town Hall but also as a magistrates court. Henry Rice designed its prominent clock tower*

The Seventh Day Adventist Church *on Castle Hill became the first in the county to represent this Protestant Christian denomination when it was dedicated in October 1958. This former Primitive Methodist Chapel became redundant and had been used as a store since 1925. It was transformed from its dilapidated state into the building we see today*

The Castle *or fortified manor is thought to date from before 1300. The king's surveys report the wall surrounding the manor house as ruinous in 1337. Extensive repairs followed and the hall was rebuilt in 1361. Following the reign of Richard II the building was totally neglected. English chronicler and antiquary, William Worcester, describes the castle as standing in 1478, but when the poet John Leland visited in 1538 only a few insignificant remains were left. It is now the site of a park and playground*

Fountain

Masonic Hall

Guildhall clock tower   *Foresters Hall*

You reach Castle Street – cross with care and follow the path opposite up Castle View. This is a short, sharp up and as it begins to flatten out you will see to your right the war memorial. Keep following the path, passing the cottages of Castle Gardens on the left and a playground atop the hill, also on the left, before bending right to descend back to Castle Street. There is a nice view ahead here down Castle Hill, but the walk turns left along Castle Street. In less than 100m you will see the lychgate over to the right leading into the churchyard of St. Martin's Church. Go through here and walk ahead to the church porch.

> Built on the site of a former Norman church, **St. Martin's Church** is the third largest in Cornwall (after Truro Cathedral and Bodmin Parish Church). It is mainly 15thC with a few earlier remains. The tower is a more modern structure having been erected to replace an earlier one demolished in 1902

St. Martin's should be worth a visit but it was locked the day we were there, so on reaching the porch, assuming you can't get in to look around, bear right on the path for a short distance to leave the churchyard via a wrought iron gate which leads onto a short lane between the lovely cottages of Church Gate. At their end turn right at the T-junction and at the next T-junction bear left along Church Street.

Pike Street

This is a road of attractive cottages – as the road bends right also spare a glance down to the lower road of Cannon Hill on the left. You pass the Grade II listed Ancient House on the right, dating from the 17thC and thought to be the oldest continuously occupied private home in town, and the late 19thC Salvation Army building on the left. At the end of Church Street turn left along Market Street again, passing Well Lane on the left, as far as the Guildhall. Here turn left along Fore Street.

About 40m along you will see a narrow path on the left leading to the Pipewell. Go down here for 25m, the 14thC well is on the left, then retrace your steps back up to Fore Street to continue in the same direction as before, noting some of the lovely shop façias. At the end of the road turn right up Pondbridge Hill and cross over to go left into Baytree Hill. Along here you find the Methodist Church on the left at the junction with Barn Street. Here turn right to go down Windsor Place back towards the town centre.

---

*The Italianate Wesleyan **Methodist Church** in Barn Street was originally built in 1846 to a design by Henry Rice. Its interior is mainly a 1907 renovation*

***Stuart House** is a late mediæval town house thought to date from 1480–1520. This large and very expensive house evolved at a time when Liskeard*

Castle was in a state of disrepair. Charles I lodged here for 4 nights when his forces were pursuing the Parliamentarians during his Cornish campaign in 1644. The building has been restored by the Stuart House Trust as an arts and heritage centre

At the mini-roundabout keep ahead on Barras Street passing Stuart House on the right followed by the beautiful County Branch Library which was originally endowed by Passmore Edwards (see note in Truro walk). Cross the road and about 25m from the library you will find the narrow Pig Meadow Lane on the left. Go down here, following it as it bends about, until it leads you into the corner of the car park.

*Before the 19thC **Pig Meadow Lane** linked Barras Street to the grounds of Westbourne House, town mansion to one of the adventurers of South Caradon Mine. It's likely that a meadow located here was bought and incorporated into the gardens which had, in a previous era, been the town's pig meadow. The rebuilding and gentrification in the mid 19thC with the influx of money from the copper mines meant the area was no longer seen as a suitable place for pigs. The lane has also been known as Coach Horse Lane after a blacksmith who had a smithy near what is now the car park and who attended to the local coach horses. The lane was partly widened to get the coaches through, as can be seen on some of the buildings. Look out for a mural depicting the history of Liskeard throughout the ages*

From here walk about 40m to the nearby bottom corner of the car park where you will find a pedestrian path to Dean Street and the Cattle Market (don't walk across the whole expanse of the car park at this point, you are only within its confines for a short distance). Follow this narrow path until you reach Dean Street. Turn right, enjoying some nice town houses for 25m until you find Westbourne Lane on the right. Go along this ancient way all the way to its junction with West Street at which point you will see the vehicular entrance to your car park along on the right.

***Westbourne Lane** is a mediæval right of way that ran through the historic gardens of Westbourne House. In the past there was a footbridge linking the gardens on both sides of the lane. Today the gardens survive on the west side only with the car park on the other. At the southern end of the lane a few houses which pre-date the mid 19thC rebuild of the town still survive today. Westbourne House at the north end now accommodates the local Social Services office*

Church

Mediæval pipewell

Stuart House

Looe

Distance: 2¾ miles / 4.5km

This walk begins with quite an unusual feature which justifies the fact that it starts through a car park (we feel!). At low tide it is a great area for spotting egrets and various other estuary birds; at high tide the views across the estuary are very picturesque. The start is close to the confluence of the East and West Looe Rivers and the walk encompasses both towns of East and West Looe. For administrative purposes the towns merged in the late 19thC to be under the jurisdiction of one governing body. East Looe has an enticing network of tiny, ancient streets and the area has been a fishing port for centuries. From here ships were sent to the Siege of Calais during the 100 Years War with France. During the walk there are a few ascents and descents which afford good views. The route is on paved paths throughout.

Start point: Footpath running alongside the Millpool Car Park and the West Looe River, PL13 2AF

Directions to start: Looe is on the south coast of Cornwall, clearly signposted on the A387

Parking: Millpool Car Park, West Looe, PL13 2AF

Public transport: Looe is served by buses from: Polperro, Plymouth, Torpoint, Liskeard etc. Bus operators include: First in Devon & Cornwall, Group Travel and Western Greyhound. Timetables available online at www.travelinesw.com. The railway station is on Station Rd, PL13 1HN

Refreshments: Café Fleur, Fore St, East Looe, 01503 265734; Rendezvous, Higher Market St, East Looe, 01503 269026

Toilets: Millpool Car Park, West Looe and near Banjo Pier, East Looe

---

Nearby places to stay: Anchor Lights, The Quay, East Looe, 01503 262334; Portwrinkle self catering apartment, Hannafore Rd, West Looe, 01579 346716; Trehaven Manor, Station Rd, East Looe, 01503 262028

Places of interest: The Eden Project, 01726 811911; Looe Island – boats trips are available and are seasonally operated by several companies in Looe; Paul Corin's Music Machines, 01579 343108; Woolly Monkey Sanctuary, Murrayton, 01503 262532

Market days: None

Authors' tip: For those who wish to stretch their legs beyond the town the coastal walk from Looe to the village of Polperro is superb

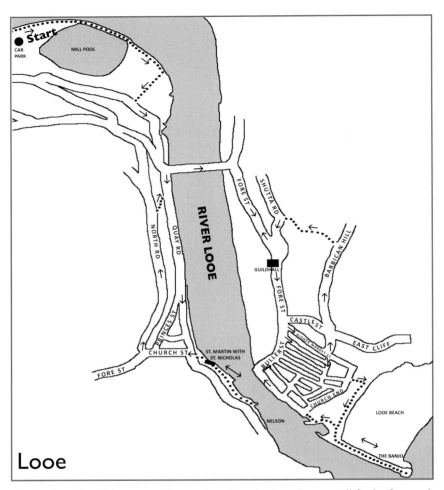

Looe

At the far side of the car park, running along its length, you will find a footpath with the West Looe River beyond it. Turn right along here, with the river to your left, and head towards the town. Soon you reach a causeway leading between the river on the left and the old mill pool on the right. This is a brief and rather diverting bit of walking – if you don't like it or it's underwater walk out of the car park at the end nearest to the town and meet us by the prominent Ambulance Station (* below).

Those on the causeway should keep ahead beyond it, following the path beside the river and past a playground. It turns right to pass the public loos and joins the road in front of the Ambulance Station (*). Turn left and follow the bends until the road leads you up to New Road. Look out for traffic and cross over with care to go down Quay Road. The bridge is to your left but we don't cross it just yet. This part of the walk is in West Looe. Follow the road beside the river, passing the United Reformed Church until you reach the tiny Parish Church of St. Martin with St. Nicholas.

The Church of St. Martin with St. Nicholas *is a bijou little church, built c. early 14thC. During its long life it has functioned as a Guildhall and schoolhouse as well as a church. Successive restorations took place during the 19th, 20th and early 21stC. The 18thC clock, having been removed in 1922, was replaced by today's replica as a Millennium Project. Notice the lovely, illuminated document hanging on the south wall*

From the church descend its steps and bear right round the building to join the path running alongside the water. Follow this until you reach the memorial statue to Nelson beyond which you can see the large arches which support the road. From Nelson retrace your steps back to the parish church and from here cross the road and walk to the left of the Community Fire Station along Church Street with its delightful cottages.

Church of St. Martin with St. Nicholas

Church Street, West Looe

Nelson *was a one-eyed, well-loved, grey seal who regularly visited Looe and became a great favourite with residents and visitors. In 2003 he ceased to visit, much to the dismay of his many fans. This life-size bronze by sculptor Suzie Marsh was unveiled by Sir Robin Knox-Johnson in 2008, a memorial to a great character and a reminder of our responsibility to the natural environment*

You emerge onto Fore Street. Glance left along this attractive road but then turn right for about 15m to enter Princes Square before turning left up North Road. You will notice the 16thC Jolly Sailor, Looe's oldest pub. Climb North Road until, just beyond the brow of the hill with its sugar almond coloured cottages on the left, you will find a footpath on the right leading back down to Quay Road. Go down here and at the bottom cross the bridge into East Looe.

The Jolly Sailor *dates from the early 16thC, is Grade II listed and was once the haunt of pirates and smugglers. Until the 19thC boats could moor alongside it but the land has now been reclaimed from the sea and cottages built on the site*

The Bridge: *The first bridge to span the river was constructed in 1411 and was made of wood. It was replaced by a stone bridge in 1436 which had 14 arches and a chapel in the centre. The Victorian bridge you see today was opened in the mid 19thC and is slightly further upstream than the original*

Nelson

West Looe cottages

At the end of the bridge turn right, passing the war memorial on the right, then keep ahead along Fore Street with shops to the left and a car park to your right. Pass the Victorian Guildhall of 1878 on your right which houses the TIC, then continue ahead through this narrow and ancient shopping street with its venerable 17thC buildings until you reach Higher Market Street on the left. Go up here, passing the 15thC Smugglers' Cott on the right and soon after that you reach the Museum.

Town Centre: *East Looe was something akin to an early 'new' town, being built on a grid layout which is evident as you explore. There are some very historic buildings dating from the 15th to 17thC. The Smugglers' Cott on Higher Market Street dates back to the first half of the 15thC and was restored in the 1590s using timbers salvaged from the Armada. A 3' high tunnel in the cellar, re-discovered in the 1930s, leads to the quay, hence the association with smuggling*

Looe Museum *dates back to the 15thC and has seen service as a gaol, magistrate's court and Guildhall during its colourful history. It still boasts many original features and is Grade II* listed. It opens seasonally*

Immediately after the Museum turn right and in 15m go left and then right again, winding your way through the buildings towards a prominent, turreted church

Museum, East Looe

Middle Market Street, East Looe

tower, glancing along the picturesque, narrow ways as you pass. When you reach the church continue past it, but first glance over your left shoulder to notice the old Church House. Walk round the church, keeping the building on your left and noticing the huge stained glass window which still exists as part of the conversion. You emerge at a car park beyond which is the promenade. Join this and turn right, with the sea to your left and notice the lovely sundial mounted on an obelisk dating from 1891. Follow the railings to their end then walk out along the Banjo Pier, so named for its shape. At the end you can glimpse Looe Island to the right, once the home of monks. The distant headland to the left across Whitsand Bay is the Rame Peninsula, 10½ miles away, with the village of Downderry slightly closer across the water.

St. Mary's Church *was dedicated in 1259 but over the centuries fell into disrepair until it was rebuilt in the early 19thC and then again in the late 19thC, retaining its 13thC style. The one-handed clock on the tower was restored in 1996. It has now been deconsecrated and is used by a housing project*

Church Houses *were the mediæval equivalent of the village hall, their main purpose having been to raise funds for the church. Often they would be venues for church ales, a celebration comprising sport, plays and Morris dancing – all enhanced by a strong beer brewed on the premises. With the rise of Puritanism such festivities were deemed inappropriate and church houses were closed. After 1600 the buildings began to see use as schools, poor houses, inns or private homes*

Leave the pier and head towards the old Lifeboat Station. As you approach you will see the new Lifeboat Station to the left, walk round the left side of this to pass its front with the river to your left. Nelson's statue is opposite you now. Walk along the Quay until it bends right into Buller Street. Follow this, enjoying glimpses along the side roads, until you reach Middle Market Street on the right. Turn down here, encountering more lovely old buildings and passing the rear of the Smugglers' Cott on your left. Keep ahead until, just before you are faced by the wall of a cottage you find the left turning which once more brings you out beside the Museum and back to Higher Market Street.

On Higher Market Street turn left and immediately right up Tower Hill. This is quite a climb, keep going, passing a staggered crossroads and continuing up Barbican Hill with its rewarding views. Despite the road names there is no evidence of fortification. In 180m you reach a footpath descending to the left. This is just before the 'Zone Ends' road signs. Go down this path enjoying the views to the left and it eventually leads to steps which emerge onto a narrow lane beside an old well. This is Shutta Road.

St. Ann's Well *was restored by the Looe Old Cornwall Society in 1977. In 2006 the gate was renewed with a legacy from Beatrice Rose Whittington, a former member of the Society, who died in 2004 aged 109. Her daughter, Kate, cut the ribbon at the opening ceremony*

Turn left here to pass the beautiful, early 20thC house of Chapel Court on your left, this is now divided into apartments. Shutta Road drops down to rejoin Fore Street near the present Guildhall. Turn right here to return to the bridge, re-cross the river and bear right back down to the car park and your starting point.

Looe view

Lostwithiel

Distance: 1 mile / 1.6km

This is a very short walk around a very delightful small town which was founded in the 12thC and is rich with history. It was once the most important stannary town in Cornwall, the tin mining industry being the major source of revenue. There is one short ascent then a descent and the walk is on good paths throughout.

Start point: The car park at Pleyber Christ Way, PL22 0HE

Directions to start: Lostwithiel stands at the head of the Fowey estuary, roughly equidistant between Fowey to the south and Bodmin to the north. The A390 runs through the town

Parking: Pleyber Christ Way (off the A390) beyond the TIC, Community Centre and Fire Station, PL22 0HE

Public transport: Lostwithiel is well served by buses from: Bodmin, St. Austell, Liskeard, Plymouth, Fowey, Callington, Truro etc. Bus operators include First in Devon & Cornwall, Roselyn Coaches and Western Greyhound. Timetables available online at www.travelinesw.com. Lostwithiel Railway Station is at Grenville Rd, PL22 0EW

Refreshments: The Duchy Coffee Shop, 10 Fore St, 01208 873184; Duchy of Cornwall Nursery Café, Cott Rd, 01208 872668; The Globe Inn, 3 North St, 01208 872501

Toilets: Church Lane

Nearby places to stay: Penrose B&B, 1 The Terrace Brookdale, 01208 871417; Tremont House, 2 The Terrace, 01208 873055; Hazelmere House, 58 Grenville Rd, 01208 873315

Places of interest: Restormel Castle (English Heritage), nr Restormel Rd, 01208 872687; Lostwithiel Museum, Fore St, 01208 873593

Market days: Farmers' Market held on Fridays every other week in the Community Centre (10am–2pm)

Authors' tip: The well-preserved Restormel Castle, administered by English Heritage, is approximately 1½ miles to the north of town and is well worth a visit

---

Leave the car park along the footpath at the end furthest away from the vehicular entrance. This short path leads you to North Street. Turn left and keep going until you reach the lovely old bridge, at which turn right. The River Fowey is to your left with a pleasant picnic area adjacent. Soon you pass the war memorial followed by the British Legion garden. This road is The Parade and before you get too far along it remember to glance back to get a good view of the bridge.

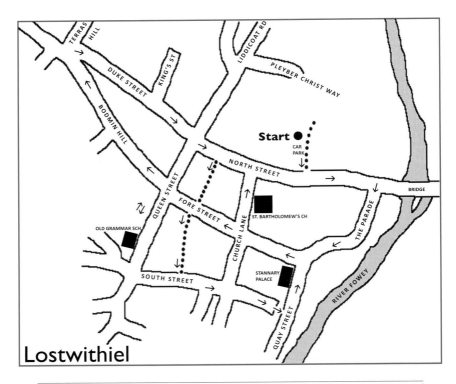

Lostwithiel

The beautiful, mostly mediæval **Bridge** *is a scheduled ancient monument and replaces an earlier wooden bridge. The first had nine arches. It has undergone many alterations over the centuries and has had to accommodate changes in the course of the river, with westerly arches becoming redundant (their foundations are now covered by the road) and easterly arches being added*

The startlingly old **Stannary Palace** *or* **Duchy Palace** *is Grade I listed and has been here for over 700 years. The buildings in existence today are the remains of a much larger complex. It was used for Duchy and stannary (tin mining) administration. The whole complex covered about two acres, stretching down Quay Street as far as the archway beneath which you will walk, and included a great hall, smelting houses and coinage hall. The last Tinners Parliament was held here in the mid 18thC and the Duchy administration relocated in the 1870s*

The road bends right and passes Parade Square on your right. Immediately after this go right up Fore Street, noticing the fabulously old Stannary Palace on your left. Fore Street is a pretty street, go past Boseglos House on the right and continue to the top of the road, admiring the many attractive buildings including the Guildhall and Museum near the top on the left and Edgcumbe House on the right. At the top of the road pause before crossing to notice the grand old building of the former Methodist Church over on the right, dating from 1900. Then cross and turn left along the main road (Queen Street) for about 50m to the Old Grammar School.

The beautiful **Boseglos House** *dates from the 18thC and is Grade II listed. It was extended in 1863 by G. E. Street who designed the Royal Courts of Justice in London*

Edgcumbe House *was built in the mid 18thC as the town house for the Edgcumbe family who came from Plymouth. It houses the mayor's parlour and although much of the building is now leased as offices several civic artefacts are still housed here. It is Grade II* listed*

The Old Grammar School *was erected by the Edgcumbes in 1781. It has also been used as a Market House. The façade you see is all that remains of the original building with apartments having been built behind it*

Lostwithiel Bridge

Retrace your steps to the crossing and go left up Bodmin Hill. About 20m up here on the left is an attractively gabled house set back from the road. This was once the old fire station and prior to that saw service as a cinema. It is now a private house. Continue up the delightful Bodmin Hill with its attractive cottages until you reach Terras Hill on the right. Turn right and immediately right again to head down Duke Street with lovely views of the countryside beyond the town ahead of you. Soon the spire of the church comes into view. Pass King's Street, the Royal Oak Inn and more pretty cottages as you descend to meet the main road again.

Cross the road and go straight ahead down North Street. Within a few metres on the right you will see the entrance to the courtyard of Taprell House. Just beyond this is the Grade II listed Old Malthouse – notice the inscribed plaque on its corner. Immediately beyond this a tiny lane, Malthouse Lane, leads back towards the Guildhall and Museum. Take this, and when you reach Fore Street cross over and continue down the lane to the right of the Museum's entrance. This leads down an ancient-feeling path, passing the old gaol and continuing beyond to emerge on South Street.

*The Tudor **Taprell House** probably dates from the 16thC and was built by the Taprell family. William Taprell, mayor during the Siege of Lostwithiel in the Civil War, lived here. The property was later bought by the Edgcumbes who*

Malthouse Lane

Fore Street

carried out major alterations. Edgcumbe House on Fore Street was built in the mid 18thC and backs onto this building. The Town Council bought Taprell House in 1934 and restored it in 1991 although many original features remain. It now houses the library and Methodist Church

The Georgian **Guildhall** was built in 1740 by Richard Edgcumbe, who later became Lord Lieutenant of Cornwall. The town council still meet here and the ground floor, which was once used as a corn market, now houses the museum. A copy of Lostwithiel's 12thC charter is displayed here. Behind the museum is an older section of the building which used to be the gaol

Turn left along South Street. Pass Church Lane and continue ahead to walk under a venerable archway, part of the old Stannary Palace. Beyond here turn left along Quay Street which is flanked by more palace remnants on the left hand side. When you reach the junction with Fore Street and The Parade go left along Fore Street. We know you've done this particular 100m before but we make no apologies as it's such a nice bit. When you reach Boseglos House again turn right along Church Lane. St. Bartholomew's is on the right.

The Grade I listed **St. Bartholomew's Church** with its noticeable spire mostly dates from the 14thC although an earlier church occupied the site. The tower beneath the spire is 13thC and in the Early English style. It is said that *during the Civil War Parliamentarians brought a horse into the church and christened him Charles*

After exploring the church continue along Church Lane to the end then turn right along North Street, walking round the corner of the churchyard. Enjoy the old townhouses along this stretch before you find the pathway on your left back into the car park.

Taprell House

Boseglos House

St. Bartholomew's Church

Walk 8
Marazion
Distance: 1.8 miles / 2.9km

Marazion derives its name from the numerous markets held here over the centuries, the first being recorded in 1070. It is one of the towns which claims to be the oldest in Britain. This walk is dominated by the dramatic and beautiful sight of St. Michael's Mount out in the bay. Although only a small town there are some gracious buildings and attractive houses. The route takes you round the rural environs where the views can be most admired. It is on good paths throughout, although the stretch along the seafront is stony in places rather than paved. There are a few, fairly gentle ascents.

Start point: Market Place, outside the Town Hall, TR17 0AR

Directions to start: Marazion is situated on the south coast in west Cornwall. It is 3 miles to the east of Penzance and is accessible from the A30 and A394

Parking: Folly Field Car Park, West End, Marazion, TR17 0EP

Public transport: Marazion is well served by buses from: Penzance, Helston, Falmouth, Truro, St. Just etc. Bus operators are First in Devon & Cornwall and Western Greyhound. Timetables available online at www.travelinesw.com. Nearest railway stations are Penzance (2.9 miles) and St. Erth (3.2 miles)

Refreshments: Delicious, Fore St, 01736 711879; The Kings Arms, The Square, 01736 710291

Toilets: The Square

Nearby places to stay: Blue Horizon, Fore St, 01736 711199; Denham House, Feliskirk Lane, 01736 719490; St. Michael's B&B, The Cornerhouse, Fore St, 01736 711348

Places of interest: St. Michael's Mount (partly administered by The National Trust), 01736 710507; Marazion Museum, Market Place, 01736 710234; Trengwainton Garden, Madron, nr Penzance 01736 363148

Market days: None

Authors' tip: No visit to Marazion would be complete without a trip to St. Michael's Mount. During the season this wonderful island can be reached either on foot via a cobbled causeway, or by boat

From the car park the coast path runs towards the town. Follow this, away from the car park with the sea wall and the sea beyond it to your right and fabulous views towards St. Michael's Mount. A grassy area with playground is to your left.

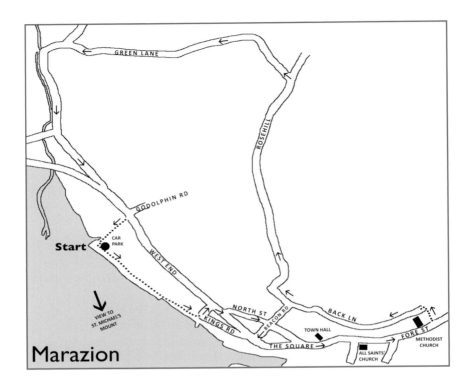

Marazion

St Michael's Mount *has been a site of religious focus since the 5th or 6thC. After the Norman Conquest the abbey was granted to the Benedictines of Mont St. Michel in France. Until the reformation many pilgrims flocked to the island, contributing to the wealth of Marazion where they had to bide their time until the tide was right for crossing. In 1588 the first beacon to warn of the approaching Armada was lit here. The Mount has seen many skirmishes over the centuries, particularly during the Civil War. The island is the historic home of the St. Aubyn family who arrived in 1647. In 1954 St. Michael's Mount was given to the National Trust but the family retained a lease to live at the castle. A small island community lives in the village on the Mount*

As you walk along this path spare a glance inland occasionally as there are some rather lovely houses over on the main road, including the pair of Dutch-gabled Rookery Lodges from 1887 and the nearby Grade II*, late 18thC house which was formerly called Trelawney House or The Rookery. This is now the Manor Office for the St. Aubyn Estates and other businesses.

Walk beside the coast path for just over 250m, passing a memorial to HMS Warspite and, further along, a building on the left which was constructed in 1907 for Marazion's working men. Just after this you reach a road leading to the ferry slipway down on the right. Go left here, this is King's Road and leads you back to the main road where you will find a Tudor-style fish and chip shop! Turn right, watching out for traffic, and take the next left along North Street, but just before you do glance a little further along the main road past Ebenezer Cottage to the now-converted, Grade II listed Ebenezer Chapel which was the Free Methodist Church dating from 1862.

HMS Warspite *was built at Devonport in Plymouth and was launched in 1913. She saw very active service in both World Wars, sustaining substantial damage on several occasions. She was sold for scrap in 1947 and ran aground in Mounts Bay during a gale on the way to the ship-breakers*

The walk continues up North Street, passing the old town well on the left. This was the main water supply for this part of town until mains water was brought in during the 1870s.

At a tiny crossroads with Beacon Road glance ahead, there are some attractive houses along here, but turn right down Beacon Road and you arrive at The

St Michael's Mount

Square. Turn left along the road, passing some gardens and the Grade II listed, 18thC White House on the right. Soon you reach Market Place with the Marazion Institute and Town Hall.

__The Marazion Institute__ dating from 1883, was built for Theophilus Code and was presented to the town in 1890 by his widow and family as a memorial to him and for use as a library

The Victorian, Grade II listed __Town Hall__ building dates from 1871. It has served various purposes during its life, including that of prison and fire station.

Town Hall

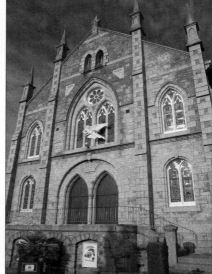

All Saints' Church   *Methodist Church*

For a time it was used by Barclays Bank. It is now home to the Museum and bears a plaque commemorating the 500 years since Queen Elizabeth I affirmed the town charter in 1595 (an earlier one had been granted in 1257 by Henry III). This provided for fairs and markets to be held on certain dates and established administrative arrangements for Marazion which prevailed until 1835

Continue ahead out of the centre of the town, slightly uphill. Glance down side roads as you go, there are some intriguing backwaters. Pass the Old Police House on the right and beyond it is the lovely All Saints' Church, which is much larger inside than you might think from the approach. Opposite the church is the war memorial.

All Saints' Church *is another lovely, Victorian building with a pretty interior, some vibrantly coloured stained glass and attractive, polygonal chancel. Also Grade II listed, the church was consecrated in 1861 although two earlier buildings occupied the site. The previous church was dedicated to St. Hermes*

Continue along Fore Street as far as the Methodist Church on the left, a Grade II listed building dating from 1893. About 30m beyond here on the left is tiny

Malthouse Lane. Go along here to reach steps which take you up to Back Lane. At the top of the steps continue ahead with glimpses of Mount's Bay to the left and, as you progress, a good view over the roofs down into the Market Place. Follow Back Lane for almost 250m until you reach a fork, at which point go left. You swiftly bend right, between houses, to reach a junction at a U-bend. Keep ahead here along Rosehill. The old cemetery is to your right (a more recent one is at the other end of town), the gravestones of which have been moved to the periphery to ease the task of mowing the grass. At the end of the cemetery wall bear right uphill and keep going for just over 0.3 mile until you reach the second turning on the left. During this stretch of the walk you have beautiful views across Mount's Bay and the surrounding countryside. Penzance is across the bay.

When you reach the second left turn, with its conveniently located bench, go left. This is just beyond a stone house called The Stitches and the road is Green Lane, although nothing tells you this. Keep following Green Lane for just over ½ mile as it bends and descends, passing some houses and gardens on the way which have a distinctly Mediterranean air. Ignore any turnings left or right but keep bending with Green Lane until you meet the main road back into town. This is West End.

Turn left along the road for 60m and cross over with care to re-enter the car park opposite Godolphin Drive.

Marazion roofscape

Padstow
Distance: 1¾ miles / 2.8km

Padstow, on the bank of the River Camel, was originally called Petroc-stowe after the Welsh missionary who came here and to whom the church is dedicated. It is a bustling harbour town with a great nautical atmosphere and some lovely town houses and cottages. Gulls mourn overhead and around your feet along with confiding little turnstones, hurrying about the quay on their red legs. There are a few ascents up behind the town but nothing too onerous. There are plenty of eating places to tempt you to pause and partake and lots of enticing backwaters along which to peer.

Start point: South Quay Car Park, Riverside, PL28 8BY

Directions to start: Padstow is situated on the west side of the Camel estuary near the north coast of Cornwall. It is 8½ miles to the NW of Wadebridge. The A389 runs through the town

Parking: South Quay Car Park, Riverside, PL28 8BY

Public transport: Padstow is served by buses from: Bodmin, Newquay, St. Columb Major, Indian Queens etc. Bus operators are First in Devon & Cornwall and Western Greyhound. Timetables available online at www.travelinesw.com. Nearest railway stations are Roche (9.6 miles), and St. Columb Road (9.7 miles)

Refreshments: Cherry Trees Coffee House, West Quay, 01841 532934; Greens Café, North Quay, 01841 534834

Toilets: In the car park adjacent to the harbour

Nearby places to stay: Althea Library B&B, 27 High St, 01841 532717; 50 Church St B&B, Padstow, 01841 532121; Treann House, 24 Dennis Rd, 01841 533855

Places of interest: Prideaux Place, Tregirls Lane, 01841 532411; Padstow Museum, The Institute, Market Place, 01841 532752

Market days: None

Authors' tip: If time allows consider taking the ferry across the River Camel to Rock. Armed with an Ordnance Survey map and suitable footwear, a mile along public footpaths will get you to the Church of St. Enodoc (Grid ref: SW932772). This is located just to the east of Brea Hill and is the resting place of Sir John Betjemen

From the car park turn right along the road. Go left round the Old Custom House on South Quay then immediately left up Strand Street. At the top turn

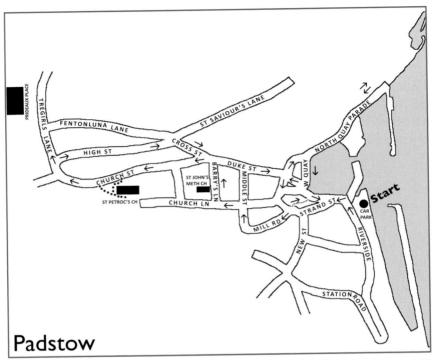

Padstow

right down Broad Street then take the next left along Mill Road. Follow Mill Road to the junction with Church Lane where you'll find Middle Street ahead, with its almshouses, and Lanadwell Street on the right with more attractive buildings. The walk goes left along Church Lane until you find Barry's Lane on the right. Go right here, passing St. John's Methodist Church, at the end go left along Duke Street, then left again on Church Street. Follow this as far as the church. Walk round the church and enter via its south door for a visit.

The Grade II listed **almshouses** *were built in 1875, one of the cottages in the complex being built as a memorial to John Tredwen, a local ship builder, who died in June 1870. They were renovated and renamed Tredwen Court in January 1989*

St. John's Methodist Church *occupies the site of a former chapel which was demolished, although the hall behind was retained and redesigned*

St. Petroc's Church *as it is today is the third church to occupy this site. A 6thC church was destroyed by Vikings in AD981 and a remnant from this time,* *in the form of a 4-holed Celtic cross, can be seen on the bank to the left of the south door. The next church was built in the 12thC and the bottom section of the tower dates from this time. The present church was built in the mid 15thC and is Grade I listed. It has little stained glass resulting in a palely lit, tranquil interior. It has a beautiful, carved Mediæval font depicting the 12 apostles*

Turn right out of the south door and follow the path ahead through the churchyard back to Church Street. Turn left, going uphill, and when Church Street bends left turn right into Tregirls Lane. Follow this, passing High Street on your right, until you reach Prideux Place. There are beautiful views across its park where you might also see fallow deer. From here return along Tregirls Lane, passing the mid 19thC Dower House at the top of Fentonluna Lane.

__Prideaux Place__ is a Grade I listed, Elizabethan manor house, home of Me Too Bear and the Prideaux-Brune family, the Prideaux having resided in Cornwall since the 11thC. This house was completed at the end of the 16thC with some remodelling during the 19thC. Many of its copious bedrooms remain in the condition in which they were left by soldiers at the end of WWII

When you reach the High Street go left down it, passing the Althea Library on the right. At the crossroads go right down Cross Street and when Church Street joins you from the right continue straight ahead. Cross Street runs into Duke

Prideaux Place

Street. Follow its raised pavement down and at the bottom turn left along Market Place. Follow the road as it bends right and leads back to the Quay.

*The **Althea Library** was built as part of the nearby Prideaux-Brune Estate and dates from the 19thC. It was originally a boys' school, then a Sunday School and subsequently became a library when the original Althea Library, located in a cottage over the road, was moved here on the retirement of its founder. The house ceased to function as a library in the 1960s*

Walk ahead along the Quay with the water to your right, passing the incredibly ancient-looking Abbey House on the left. Pass the Red Brick Building which houses the TIC and keep going until you reach the pier. Go along it to visit its little pill box and admire the views. There are no railings, don't drop off. Rock is the village across the water.

*The 15thC **Abbey House** was originally a guild headquarters for Padstow merchants. It is a private house and is Grade II* listed*

***Pill Box:** This reminder of WWII is now used as a store by the harbour. Others used to exist here but have been demolished, although some remnants are still visible along the estuary*

Typical Padstow

Along the Quay – Abbey House far right

Return along the pier and go left. Notice a Big Pin standing proudly on the opposite headland of Dennis Hill. Follow the Quay as it goes left and before it turns left again at the far side of the boats go right along the narrow Market Strand. In 30m turn left along Market Place, passing the Padstow Institute and Museum building on the right.

The Dennis Hill Obelisk *is a Grade II listed building commemorating the golden jubilee of Queen Victoria in 1887. It was built in 1889*

The Padstow Museum, *housed on the first floor of the Padstow Institute building, was founded by local volunteers in 1971. It is a mine of local information and well-worth visiting. Two of its exhibits are the Little Horsemen of Padstow who were found during the re-roofing of Barclays Bank.* **The Padstow Institute** *was built in 1881 as a working men's club to encourage "social intercourse, mutual helpfulness, mental and moral improvement, and rational recreation". It is Grade II listed*

Keep ahead and at the junction with Lanadwell Street on the right go left up Broad Street. In less than 40m, just before the junction, go left down the cobbled Drang. This takes you back to the Quay. From here bear right, retracing your steps back round the Old Custom House and thence to the car park.

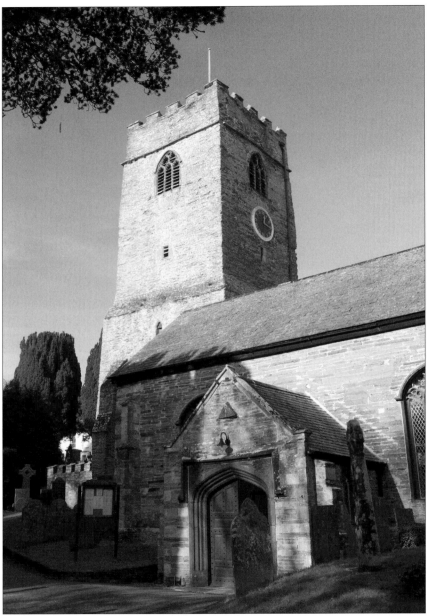

St. Petroc's, Padstow

Wadebridge
Distance: 2¾ miles / 4.5km

Wadebridge straddles the River Camel and before the construction of the bridge was known simply as 'Wade'. At that time the river was crossed by means of a ford. This was a very risky undertaking and many people and animals perished. Chapels on each bank provided a place to pray before crossing – an early kind of travel insurance. This walk starts away from the centre of Wadebridge on Egloshayle Road. It is a fairly level walk, mostly on pavements although the few rougher paths which you will encounter are still quite comfortable underfoot.

Start point: Egloshayle Rd at the junction of Trenant Vale, PL27 6AE

Directions to start: Wadebridge is situated between Padstow and Bodmin in north Cornwall. It is easily accessible from both the A39 and the A389

Parking: On-street parking at Egloshayle Rd close to the junction of Trenant Vale, PL27 6AE

Public transport: Wadebridge is well served by buses from: Port Isaac, Bodmin, Truro, Exeter, Camelford, Boscastle, St. Columb Major etc. Bus operators include First in Devon & Cornwall, Group Travel, Travel Cornwall and Western Greyhound. Timetables available online at www.travelinesw.com. Nearest railway stations are Roche (6.8 miles), Bugle (8.3 miles) and Bodmin Parkway (9.1 miles)

Refreshments: Relish Food and Drink, Foundry Court, 01208 814214; The Shed Café and Breakfast Bar, 1, Trevanson St, 07540 125832

Toilets: Egloshayle Rd (nr tennis courts) and Palmorla Rd

Nearby places to stay: Pawton Stream Boutique B&B, St. Breock, 01208 814845; Brookdale B&B, Trevanion Rd, 01208 815425

Places of interest: Camel Valley Vineyards, Nanstallon, Bodmin, 01208 77959; The John Betjeman Centre, Southern Way, 01208 812392; Pencarrow House and Gardens, nr Camelford, 01208 841369

Market days: Country Market in the Town Hall, The Platt, every Thursday from 8.45am to 12.30pm

Authors' tip: Just 3½ miles south west of town the St. Breock Downs Monolith (English Heritage) can be reached off an unclassified road to Rosenannon. Standing near the summit of St. Breock Downs and weighing in at 16½ tons this is the largest and heaviest of Cornwall's prehistoric monoliths. There are wonderful views from here

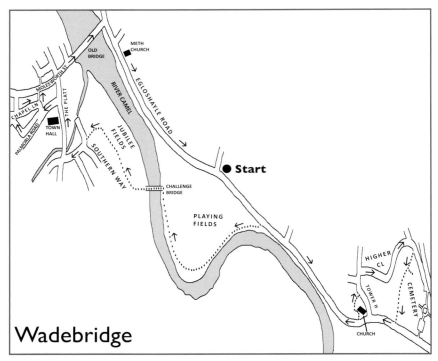

Wadebridge

Walk along Egloshayle Road with houses to your left, playing fields to your right and lovely views further right to the hills beyond the town. Soon the river bends into view on your right and you will see the church tower ahead of you. Keep walking along this road until you reach Egloshayle Church on the left. Enter here for a look around.

> **Egloshayle Church:** *A church is thought to have existed on this site since the 12thC. Egloshayle, the name of the village in which it is situated, means church by the river and it is dedicated to St. Petroc. Today's impressive interior includes a carved pulpit of 15thC Caen stone and a relatively modern east window dating from 1932. Rumour has it that the 15thC tower was constructed using surplus money and stone from the old bridge*

Leave the church and turn right out of the porch along the gravel path. This leads through the churchyard to a gateway onto Tower Hill. Follow this past the Shuttleworth Memorial Hall on the left and just beyond here turn right along Higher Close. There are some pretty cottages in this area which was once a village on its own, quite separate from Wadebridge. Pass the Earl of St. Vincent

Inn and Molesworth Cottages, following the road as it bends about until you reach a T-junction.

Turn right and you swiftly find a gate on the right into the attractive and old-feeling Wadebridge Cemetery. If you are adequately shod go through here and follow the grassy path through the graves, looking out for local moggies, until another gate leads you to a walled path out of the cemetery and back to Egloshayle Road. For those wishing to stay on solid paths, don't go through the first gate into the graves but instead keep ahead on a tarmac footpath until you reach another gate, this time leading through the more modern part of the cemetery on hard paths and back to Egloshayle Road.

Egloshayle Church

However you get back to Egloshayle Road, when you reach it turn right back towards the town, passing the church on your right. The river comes in close to the road and just after it bends away again look out for an entrance into the playing fields on your left. This gives access to a path through this pleasant area, with the river to your left and soon some rather splendid conifer trees on your right. Also, glance back for a nice view of the church. Follow the path to the modern suspension bridge and cross the river on it, enjoying its slight bounce and the views downriver to the right towards the old bridge with the straight lines of the modern road bridge beyond.

Challenge Bridge: *This impressive suspension footbridge spans the River Camel and links the playing fields of Egloshayle on one side to the Jubilee Fields on the other. Officially called Bailey Bridge, locals often refer to it as Challenge Bridge as it was constructed in 1991 by Anneka Rice and her team for the TV series "Challenge Anneka"*

At the end of the bridge keep straight ahead on the path through the area known as the Jubilee Fields, leaving the river behind. When you reach a car park bear left out of the fields and at the car park's vehicular exit keep straight ahead (first noticing the old station building off to the left on Southern Way), passing the

Challenge Bridge   Town Hall clock

Old Railway Station

library on your left. You're back amongst traffic here so watch your step. In 100m you reach a mini roundabout with The Regal Cinema opposite. This screened its first film in 1930 when it was called the Cinedrome. Here turn right along The Platt, crossing a small bridge and heading towards the town centre.

The Old Railway Station: *The last train departed from Wadebridge on 28th January 1967 following railway cutbacks. In 1989 this old building was converted from its derelict state and has housed the John Betjeman Centre since 1991. Betjeman himself would often arrive here on a steam train from Waterloo Station in London and travel on from here to Trebetherick by horse and cart. Trebetherick is a village 6 miles north of Wadebridge which Betjeman visited frequently as an adult having enjoyed many family holidays here as a youngster*

Pass the Town Hall with its clock tower and just after that an inn called Bridge on Wool. Go left after this along Palmorla Road for about 50m until you reach a right hand fork leading you up Foundry Terrace. Go up here bending right after 90m, right again after 40m and right again after another 15m to descend the narrow Chapel Lane (there is no road name, you'll need to believe us). There are more attractive cottages on this loop which is why we bring you here! Another 90m brings you to the bottom of Chapel Lane where the road bends right and you find Foundry Court on your right, an attractive precinct of shops and cafés. If you're not going in here to partake turn left at the bend, off Chapel Lane and along a short, pedestrianised road called Foundry Street. This leads to Molesworth Street.

The Town Hall: *Originally known as Molesworth Hall this building was officially opened by Sir Paul Molesworth in 1888. It was completed at a cost of the then princely sum of £3,000. The façade changed in 1962 when the run down premises underwent renovation. There is a mural which depicts the old bridge on the back wall of a stage within. The building now houses the Town Council offices*

The walk now continues right along Molesworth Street but first we recommend you detour left to visit one of our favourites, The Wadebridge Bookshop, one of the top 50 independents in the country. Continuing back down Molesworth Street, keep ahead at the crossroads with The Platt and Eddystone Road and soon you reach the old bridge over the river. Cross here, with the modern bridges to left and right along the river, and at the end of the bridge go right. This is Egloshayle Road again. Pass the Methodist Church on the left and continue along the road back to the tennis courts and your starting point.

The old bridge

Molesworth Street

Eddystone Road: *In 1882 stonemasons began work on a replacement to the damaged Eddystone Lighthouse (13 miles SW of Plymouth). Granite quarried from the nearby De Lank quarry was prepared in this area of Wadebridge before being shipped to Eddystone Rocks where the new construction was assembled. This became the 4th Eddystone Lighthouse and is still in use today*

The Old Bridge: *Reverend Thomas Lovibond, vicar of Egloshayle, grew increasingly distressed at the number of fatalities occurring during attempted crossings of the River Camel to Wade. To address this problem he planned the construction of a bridge and, under his supervision, work commenced in 1460 until its completion 8 years later. During the English Civil War in 1646, Oliver Cromwell, aware of the bridge's strategic importance, descended on it with his army of 1,500 soldiers to successfully assume control. It is said that the bridge is built on wool thus influencing the name of the "Bridge on Wool" pub in the town. A more plausible theory is that profits from the wool trade financed the bridge. The bridge once had seventeen arches, but today only fourteen remain. It is 97.5m long*

Newquay
Distance: 4.3 miles / 7km

Newquay is a town of contrasts. Once a small, mediæval fishing village called Towan Blystra, meaning something along the lines of 'windblown dunes', the 'new quay' was built during the 15thC and the town's history centred on the fishing and boat building industries. Nowadays it is renowned for its surfing. You will see much evidence of this, not least along the beach where it's great to sit and watch the exhilarating activities. Because of the Gannel Estuary, which you follow along part of the walk, it's also excellent for birdlife. For an urban area there are lots of footpaths on the walk, most of them tarmac but a few may be a little rough and stony so flat shoes (girls) are necessary. You will also enjoy public gardens, a busy harbour (the present one dates from the 19thC) and a smattering of history. There are quite a few ascents and descents.

Start point: At Holy Trinity Roman Catholic Church, Tower Rd, TR7 1LS

Directions to start: Newquay is on the north Cornwall coast, 13 miles north of Truro. Roads lead off the A30 and A39 into the town

Parking: Belmont Car Park, Toby Way (off Tower Rd), TR7 1HG

Public transport: Newquay is well served by buses from: Falmouth, Truro, Camelford, Okehampton, Exeter, St. Austell, St. Ives, Padstow etc. Bus operators include First in Devon & Cornwall and Western Greyhound. Timetables available online at www.travelinesw.com. Newquay Railway Station is located at Station Parade, TR7 2NF

Refreshments: The Beached Lamb Café, 72–74 Fore St, 07855 775782; Fort Inn, 63 Fore St, 01637 875700; Lakeside Café, Newquay Boating Lake, Trenance Lane, 01637 872703

Toilets: Trenance Gardens, East St and Fore St

Nearby places to stay: Headland Hotel, Fistral Beach, 01637 872211; Hepworth Hotel, 27 Edgcumbe Ave, 01637 873686; Westward B&B, 25 Edgcumbe Ave, 01637 871627

Places of interest: Lappa Valley Steam Railway, St. Newlyn East, 01872 510317; Trerice (National Trust), Kestle Mill, nr Newquay, 01637 875404

Market days: There is a small traditional market at Chester Rd, TR7 3BP (Monday–Saturday)

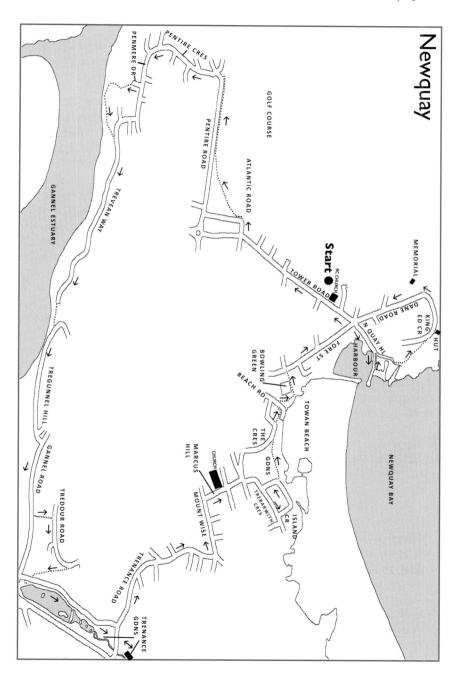

Newquay

Authors' tip: For the ornithologists amongst you make sure to bring your binoculars. The beautiful River Gannel estuary is home to many species of wading birds including curlew and oystercatcher

From the Catholic Church on Tower Road turn right along the road. Notice the terraced houses opposite the church with their attractive tiled gables – the final house having quirkily replaced theirs with the head of a great white shark. Follow Tower Road for ¼ mile, passing the castellated club house of Newquay Golf Club on the right, originally a grand house built for the Molesworth family in 1835. When you reach Atlantic Road on the right go down here and as the road bends left go through a gate ahead then turn left along the path beyond. Follow this as it skirts the golf course on your right.

At its end the path goes left to lead you out to a junction of roads. Cross straight over and walk ahead along Pentire Crescent, passing modern, gated houses on the left. Keep along Pentire Crescent for nearly 300m until you find a left turn into Penmere Drive. There are nice views here, take the first turning right, still called Penmere Drive, and at the end of this short stretch of road, you find a footpath heading down towards the estuary. Follow this as it drops down passing garden fences to the left and trees to the right. The path bends left with the river down to your right, keep along it until it opens out into a grassy area. Here bear left across the grass to the road, Trevean Way, at which turn right through this attractive residential area. The road ends and a footpath continues. There is a picnic area near here above the estuary and the site of the 19thC Gannel Boatyard – a brilliant spot for bird watching.

Follow the path and it leads to a road opposite Tregunnel House. Turn right downhill passing a small area of car park. There is an information board here about the Gannel Estuary and a handy bench. Continue until you reach the junction with the main road and turn right along it, keeping to the right-hand pavement for less than 200m. There are good views over the river plains to the right here, try not to notice the traffic on the left! As the river on the right meanders in to meet you, you have an option. Those wishing to avoid a climb and a stony path should continue along the main road until you find the public gardens on the left with their boating lake and ornamental fountain. Then continue from (*) below.

Those not minding a flight of steps and a rough, but attractive, leafy path should cross over, with care. You will see a footpath signed 'To the town' off the road on the left. Take this, walking away from the road and up steps – quite a lot of steps. The steps lead up to a road (Tredour Road, though nothing tells you), turn right along the road, ignoring the path which continues opposite.

In about 70m look out for the path off this road going right back on yourself, a sign says 'leading to Rawley Lane'. Follow this, it can be rough underfoot, and keep going down until you reach a road with the railings of Trenance Gardens opposite. Cross over, bearing right for about 10m, and enter the gardens.

(*) Once in these delightful gardens turn left and walk through them, enjoying the birds, the plants, the refreshment stop overlooking the lake with its magnificent swan sculpture. Emerge from the gardens, cross Trenance Road on the pedestrian crossing and go straight into the continuation of the gardens on the opposite side. This is a 'there and back' bit but is worth doing. In this part of the gardens you will find the lovely old Trenance Cottages and a good view of the viaduct.

__Trenance Cottages__ are Grade II listed and in recent years have been the subject of much fund raising to ensure that they are restored. They are owned by the Borough Council which also owns the gardens. Dating from the late 18thC they pre-date the gardens and the railway. The cottages were originally a malthouse before coming into residential use in the mid 19thC. They were lived in until the 1960s when they became a museum. Little has happened to

Tidal bridge, Gannel Estuary

Trenance Gardens

alter them since then. At the time of writing restoration work was underway. **Trenance Gardens** themselves have received a facelift to celebrate 2012's Diamond Jubilee. The gardens were established during the 20thC, the lake being dug during the Great Depression of the 1930s to create employment

Trenance Viaduct: This branch line of the Newquay Railway was originally a horse-drawn tramway running between Newquay and lead mines at East Newlyn. It was opened in 1849 and was made of wood, supported on stone piers. In 1874 the piers were raised and wrought iron girders were installed so that locomotives could use it. The viaduct subsequently altered again in 1939. It is Grade II listed

When you've had enough of this leave by the gate you entered near the crossing and turn right up Trenance Road for just over 0.3 mile. This is an uphill stretch along a residential road. You crest the hill and the sea is ahead of you. Begin to descend until you reach Mount Wise on the left. Turn left here, it was on this road that William Golding was born, and follow the road for 175m until you find Marcus Hill on the right. Go down here, passing the lofty, modern Church of St. Michael the Archangel on the left.

William Golding, author of Lord of the Flies (and English teacher to the step-father of one of the authors of this book), was born on Mount Wise in *what is now the Blenheim Hotel (no. 47). This is further along the road from Marcus Hill and a blue plaque commemorates him. He spent much of his life away from Cornwall but returned during retirement. He died near Truro in 1993*

The Church of St. Michael the Archangel *was established on this site in 1911. It was rebuilt in 1996 after an arson attack in 1993 and is a graceful, modern building. At the time of our visit access inside wasn't possible, not surprisingly its security seems tight. No one was ever charged with the crime*

Continue down Marcus Hill, passing the 19thC former Methodist Chapel and adjacent Oddfellows' Hall on the right. These buildings are now converted for business use. At the bottom there is a meeting of ways at a shopping area. Cross over, bearing slightly right, to continue down Trebarwith Crescent, first noticing over on the right the original Fat Willy's Surf Shack, the one which started the world craze. Bear right with Trebarwith Crescent and take the <u>second</u> left into Island Crescent (the first left is also Island Crescent). Follow Island Crescent as it bends left, from here you can look ahead to the Huer's Hut on the headland opposite, you will be there later. As the crescent continues, look for the lovely town houses with attractive wrought ironwork on the left of the road and the fabulously located house on rocky Jago's Island above Towan Beach, reached by

Analemmatic sundial at ten past one

War memorial

a little suspension bridge. As Island Crescent goes left again, back towards Trebarwith Crescent, go right off the road to walk through public gardens, keeping ahead along the path with the beach below to your right. This is another attractive stretch with a good view across to the harbour. Look out for the millennium, analemmatic sundial on the right of the path – try it out if it's sunny!

The path leads to steps, go up them and follow the tarmac path, there is an aquarium down to your right and grass to your left with buildings beyond it. The path reaches the road, keep ahead with the beach still down to your right and in about 20m the road bends left but you leave the road and go down steps, in roughly the same direction as before, beach still to the right.

At the bottom of the steps keep ahead for about 20m then turn left to reach a small car park and walk out to the road. Cross the road and opposite the car park's vehicular entrance you will find a couple of steps leading to an ascending path. Go up here, the sea is still to your right, and the path leads you to steps going up to the left. Ascend these and at the top keep ahead to then go up more steps. At the top of these walk through the car park, skirting the public loos, to reach the road. This is Fore Street.

Go right here, noting the nice old cottages which you pass on the right and the mighty war memorial ahead on the hillside. At the mini roundabout turn right down North Quay Hill with a lovely view across the bay. Keep descending with the road and at the fork go right, you're heading down into the bustling harbour now. Look out for the steps going up to the left as you descend as you will need these when you've had enough of the boats and lobster pots.

Go up the steps just mentioned and at the top turn left and follow the railings out to the road – there are benches along here if you wish for a breather. At the road turn right, going uphill and in 75m you reach an attractive house, skirt round it with the house on your left for about 20m to some steps up to the left. As you climb these look back for good views across the bay to town. At the top of the steps continue ahead on the rough path which leads you to the Huer's Hut. There are glorious views from here – look left towards the old life boat station and coastguard's lookout on the headland. From the Huer's Hut continue along the road with the grand edifice of the Headland Hotel ahead. There is no pavement so be cautious. The road bends left and on the hill to the right of the road you will see the war memorial.

The Huer's Hut *is reminiscent of an era when pilchard fishing was a vital part of the local commerce. A lookout, or 'huer', would stay in here watching for*

Jago's Island, note Huer's Hut in background

Harbour

the arrival of the pilchard shoals which he could see from this vantage point. His cry of "heva" would alert the fishing fleet who would then receive directions from the huer as to the exact whereabouts of the fish so that they knew where to cast their nets. There has probably been a hut here since mediæval times although this building is later. It is from this tradition that the expression "hue and cry" originates

The War Memorial *is on the site of a former, ancient admiralty lookout. This impressive memorial was unveiled in 1921 by the Duke of Cornwall for those who fell in WWI, but it continues to serve as a monument to those who have died in subsequent wars*

Continue along the road, passing the Atlantic Hotel on the left and dropping down. Pass Headland Road on the right and when you reach the mini roundabout again take the second right off it along Tower Road. This quickly leads you back up to the Catholic Church from whence you started.

Huer's Hut

Walk 12
Truro
Distance: 1.6 miles / 2.6km

Truro's early history centred on its Norman Castle (which no longer exists), its port and the tin mining industry. Its life has changed over the centuries and the bustling city you see today is an attractive mix of historic and modern, gracious Georgian and Victorian buildings cheek by jowl with contemporary architecture. Some of this you will see on the walk along with public gardens and attractive town cottages and houses. The relatively young cathedral provides a graceful centrepiece and there are some very tempting restaurants. Truro sits at the confluence of two rivers, the Kenwyn and the Allen, which join to become the River Truro. The walk is level, apart from exploring Victoria Gardens, and on good paths. If you have time to stay in Truro and explore beyond this route there is much more to see.

Start point: Outside the City Hall on Boscawen St, TR1 2NE

Directions to start: Truro is situated in the centre of Cornwall. It is 11½ miles to the north of Falmouth and 13 miles to the south of Newquay

Parking: Car parks are plentiful in and around the city

Public transport: Truro is well served by buses from most locations around the county. Bus operators include First in Devon & Cornwall, Travel Cornwall, Western Greyhound. Timetables available online at www.travelinesw.com. Truro Railway Station is located on Station Road, TR1 3HH

Refreshments: Olive Eatery, 15 Kenwyn St, 01872 278258; One Eyed Cat, 116 Kenwyn St, 01872 222122; 108 Coffee House, 108c Kenwyn St, 01872 260562

Toilets: Green St and Victoria Park

Nearby places to stay: The Laurels, Penweathers, 07794 472171; South Penarth B&B, St. Clements Hill, 01872 274949; Tor Vean B&B, Kenwyn Rd, 01872 271766

Places of interest: Royal Cornwall Museum, River St, 01872 272205; Trelissick Gardens (National Trust), Feock, 01872 762090; Trewithen Gardens, Grampound Rd, Nr. Truro, 01726 883647; Truro Cathedral, 14 St. Mary's St, 01872 276782

Market days: The Farmers' Market is held every Wednesday (9am–2pm) and Saturday (9am–4pm) at The Piazza, Lemon Quay. Also

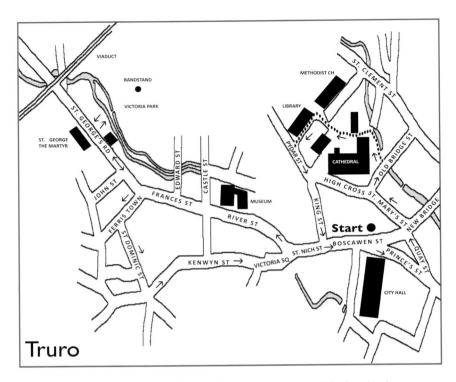

Truro

worth visiting are Lemon Street Market and Pannier Market, both open 6 days a week

Authors' tip: Every Sunday afternoon during the summer months brass bands play at the bandstand in Victoria Park

With your back to the 19thC, Grade II listed City Hall turn right to walk along Prince's Street passing the imposing Coinage Hall on your left, now a place to eat. You pass the Mansion House on your right, currently housing an estate agent, and the entrance to the Pannier Market. Also, notice the attractive slate-hung houses on the left.

The Coinage Hall is mid 19thC and was built, to house the Cornish Bank, on the site of a mediæval coinage hall where tin was brought to be assayed and taxed. The word 'coinage' derives from the French word for 'corner' as a corner of the tin was cut off to be assessed. John Wesley preached here on occasions during the 18thC

The Mansion House, *dating from the 1760s, is regarded as one of the finest Georgian houses in Cornwall. It is Grade 11* listed. The Bath stone for the building was given as a wedding present to Thomas Daniel and Elizabeth Elliot who were married in 1754. It took 7 years to build their house*

Just beyond these houses go left and almost immediately left again to walk up Quay Street with a view of the cathedral ahead. At the end of Quay Street, where you can see the other side of the Coinage Hall to your left, cross over and walk straight ahead along St. Mary's Street towards the cathedral. Pass the former, Grade II listed Grammar School on the right and when you reach the back corner of the cathedral go right along Old Bridge Street for 50m. You reach the old St. Mary's Sunday School which pre-dates the cathedral, turn left just before it to go along Wilkes Walk. You'll find yourself walking round the back of the cathedral with the River Allen on your right, on a path between palings.

After another 50m, at the end of the palings, go left to follow the path round the side of the cathedral with the buildings of the former Truro Cathedral School on your right, built in 1908 but closed as a school in the 1980s. Just beyond the old school go right at the fork of paths to quickly reach a T-junction. In front of

Coinage Hall   *St. Mary's Wesleyan Schools*

you is the beautiful building of the 1830s Methodist Church with some glorious stained glass windows. Look right to see the inscribed facia of St. Mary's Wesleyan Schools (a later 19thC addition behind the Methodist Church) but turn left and keep ahead along the pedestrianised road passing the Passmore Edwards Library on the right. This is Union Place.

John Passmore Edwards *was born in Cornwall. The son of a carpenter, he became very successful in business. He dedicated his life to charitable works, funding many educational establishments, hospitals and art galleries. He was twice offered a knighthood but turned it down on each occasion. This lovely, late 19thC building is constructed in Plymouth limestone with Bath stone dressings. It is Grade II listed*

Turn left at the end through the shopping area of Pydar Street. This has some rather lovely nooks and crannies off it which you might like to explore. You reach the attractive courtyard in front of the cathedral. Take time to visit it.

Truro Cathedral *was built in the Gothic style on the site of the 16thC St. Mary's Church. Building work started in 1880 and was completed in 1910. An elegant building, it is one of the few cathedrals in the country to have three spires. The south aisle of the old St. Mary's Church is incorporated into the body of this cathedral*

The Passmore Edwards Building

Bandstand, Victoria Gardens

After leaving the cathedral ignore the street to the left, High Cross, and turn left along King Street, a continuation of Pydar Street. At the end of King Street turn right along the main road, St. Nicholas Street, for 70m to where the road forks, then go right along River Street. Along here on the right you pass the Royal Cornwall Museum. Keep ahead beyond it to continue along Frances Street then, when the main road swings left, keep ahead along St. George's Road. Ahead you will see the lofty railway viaduct, carrying the main London to Penzance line.

__The Royal Cornwall Museum__ is the largest in Cornwall. It is housed in a building dating from 1845 which was originally built to accommodate the Truro Savings Bank. The building also contains the Courtney Library. Both the museum and library are owned by the Royal Institution of Cornwall which was founded in 1818 "for the promotion of knowledge....especially in relation to Cornwall"

Part of the Cornwall Railway, __Truro Viaduct,__ together with others along the line, was built to a design by Isambard Kingdom Brunel. These viaducts were very high maintenance and were replaced in the late 19thC / early 20thC, although the piers of the originals can often still be seen alongside, as is the case here. Truro's viaduct was the last of these replacements and is the longest in Cornwall, a striking monument to industrial architecture. It was built in 1904

You reach the building of St. Michael's Catholic School on the right, a former Methodist Church which closed in 1996 (there are plans to relocate this school). Just beyond this is the entrance into public gardens. Take time to wander round this tranquil area. The path first winds through the lower Waterfall Gardens from which you can ascend to the more formal gardens and bandstand area of Victoria Gardens. The river here is the Kenwyn.

Victoria Gardens *were designed to celebrate the diamond jubilee of Queen Victoria in 1897. They were opened in 1898. They are of a typically 19thC formal layout. Look out for the lodge commemorating the coronation of Edward VII and the fountain to mark Queen Victoria's 81st birthday. The adjacent* **Waterfall Gardens** *were opened in 1893*

Leave the Gardens and return to the entrance on St. George's Road. The Church of St. George the Martyr is opposite. Turn left to retrace your steps to the main road, passing John Street on the right. At the junction turn right into Ferris Town. In 50m go left down St. Dominic Street to its end, then go left into Kenwyn Street with a lovely view of the cathedral ahead along this rather village-like street. Keep on towards the town centre. You reach Victoria Square, keep going and this will bring you back to Boscawen Street, which in the middle ages comprised two streets, demolished at the end of the 18thC to create the more open street of today. Your start point at City Hall is on the right.

The Church of St. George the Martyr *occupies the site of a 13thC Dominican friary, from which the nearby St. Dominic Street derives its name. The dissolution of the monasteries brought an end to the friary. The present church was built in the mid 19thC*

Kenwyn Street

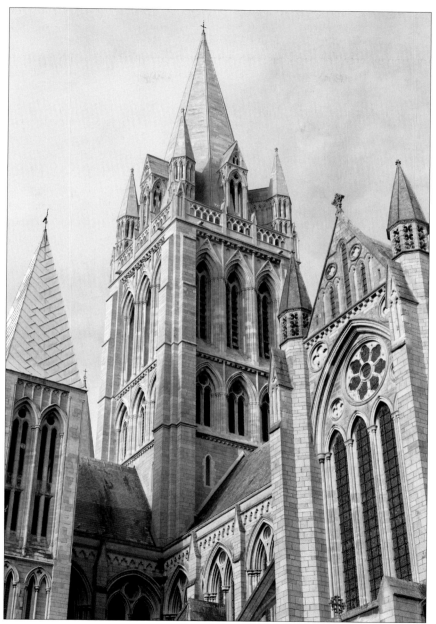

Truro Cathedral

Walk 13
Penzance
Distance: 2 miles / 3.2km

The name Penzance derives from two Cornish words which translate as 'Holy Headland' – a chapel once stood on the headland beyond the present harbour and a holy well was on the site of the parish church. In 1595 Penzance, along with other towns and villages in the area, came under attack from Spanish seafarers, part of the centuries-old battle between Protestants and Catholics. The walk around the town offers great variety: elegant residential areas, sub-tropical gardens, the quayside and plentiful shops in some wonderful, historic buildings – all to the accompaniment of the plaintive cry of gulls. This is mostly level walking on good paths, although there is a stretch of ascent up Abbey Hill. You have a great choice of places to stop for refreshment.

Start point: Market House at junction with Greenmarket and Market Jew St, TR18 2JA

Directions to start: Penzance is the most westerly town in Cornwall. It lies on the south coast some 27 miles south west of Truro and 8 miles south west of St. Ives on the north coast. It is easily accessible from the A30

Parking: Penalverne Car Park, Penalverne Drive, TR18 2RQ

Public transport: Penzance is well served by buses from: Helston, Falmouth, Truro, Mousehole, St. Just, St. Ives, Camborne, Redruth, Hayle etc. Bus operators are First in Devon & Cornwall and Western Greyhound. Timetables available online at www.travelinesw.com. Penzance Railway Station is located at Wharf Rd, TR18 2LT

Refreshments: The Honey Pot, 5 Parade St, 01736 368686; The Taj Mahal Indian and Nepalese Restaurant, 63 Daniel Place, 01736 366630

Toilets: In the car park

Nearby places to stay: Glencree House, 2 Mennaye Rd, 01736 362026; Panorama Guest House, Chywoone Hill, Newlyn, 01736 360798; Venton Vean B&B, Trewithen Rd, 01736 351294

Places of interest: Trengwainton Garden (National Trust), Madron, 01637 875404

Market days: Country Market held every Thursday at St. John's Hall, Alverton St, 8.30am–12.30pm. Farmers' Market at the same location every Friday, 9am–2pm

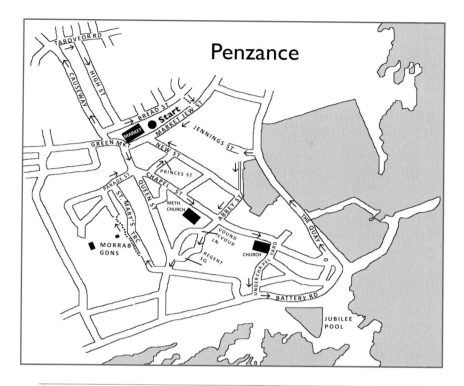

Authors' tip: Consider a trip to the Scillies. You can fly there from Penzance heliport with British International Helicopters, 01736 363871

Start from the imposing Market House in the town centre with the statue of Sir Humphry Davy. Leave him, walking along the raised pavement with the Market House on your left and shops to the right. At the end of the building go left, crossing the junction, and walk ahead down Greenmarket towards The Globe, 100m away. At The Globe go left down Chapel Street towards the church tower. This is a street with many historic and remarkable buildings – look up and around you. One particularly arresting sight is The Egyptian House on the right.

The Market House, *built in 1838 to replace an older building, dominates Market Jew Street. The street name derives from the Cornish for 'Thursday Market'*

Sir Humphry Davy *was a British chemist and inventor, born in Penzance, who is best known for his invention of the Davy Lamp – a lamp which could* *be safely used by miners in the presence of flammable gasses underground. His secretary and laboratory assistant was Michael Faraday who went on to achieve fame in his own right. Davy died in Switzerland in 1829*

Pass the grand Methodist Church on the right and The Chocolate House on the left. When you reach St. Mary's Church it's worth a visit. The graveyard has an unusually tropical feel to it with lovely sea views. Beyond the church go right off Chapel Street along Under Chapel Yard.

Chapel Street *one of the oldest surviving streets of the town, was home to Maria Branwell, mother of the Bronte sisters. It is groaning with fascinating buildings. Particularly eye-catching is the Grade I listed **Egyptian House**. Two cottages existed on the site during the 1830s and these were bought by a bookseller and mineralogist who raised their height and embellished them to create the extraordinary façade we see today. The **Methodist Church** was built in 1814 and enlarged in 1864. It has a similar interior plan to Wesley's chapel in London. The **Chocolate House**, from around 1700, was once a thatched, fisherman's cottage before serving as a confectioner's shop during the 19thC. The name derives from its more recent use as a source of hand-made chocolates with adjoining café. It is now a holiday cottage. **St. Mary's Church** was built in 1835, replacing St. Mary's Chapel which once stood here*

Humphry Davy   Market House

and from which a few relics remain including the alms box. A fire in 1985 destroyed a substantial part of the interior including the altar. The restoration is a sympathetic mix of modern and older architecture

At the seafront go left, passing the Jubilee Pool on the right with the nearby war memorial and over to the left the old Sailors' Institute Mission, built in 1908 and now holiday accommodation. Continue ahead, Mount's Bay is to your right with views to St. Michael's Mount and you are afforded occasional glimpses along intriguing side roads to your left. In about 0.3 mile you reach a swing bridge. Cross this, noticing the old lifeboat building beyond, and then go immediately left and left again along a cobbled area, Abbey Slip. Notice the small lighthouse out to the left. The church tower is up ahead of you. Climb the cobbled pavement and steps up the right hand side to reach Abbey Street.

*The **Jubilee Pool** was opened in 1935, silver jubilee year of George V, on a site traditionally used as a swimming place. It was built to withstand the elements to which it is exposed and is a Grade II listed building*

*The **Old Lifeboat House** was built in 1884 and housed the lifeboat until c. 1917. Penzance was the first Cornish port to have its own lifeboat in 1803*

Egyptian House   St. Mary's Church

Abbey Slip

At the top of the steps keep ahead passing the rather striking Abbey Hotel on the right. At the small crossroads with Chapel Street, with The Admiral Benbow on the right, cross over and keep straight ahead along Voundevour Lane. Within 100m the road forks. Keep left here along the picturesque Regent Square and follow the road through this area as it bends about and leads you out to Queen Street. Here notice the old National School building on the right, the second to be built in Penzance, then turn left and within a few metres go right along St. Mary's Terrace – there is a sign on the wall saying 'To the gardens'. As this road bends right you will find the entrance to Morrab Gardens on the left. Enter here and explore the gardens if you wish, although the walk route is along the path beyond the gate which runs adjacent to St. Mary's Terrace which is on the other side of the garden boundary to the right.

The Abbey Hotel *was built in the 17thC as a private house. It was modernised in the early 19thC in a Georgian Gothic style and became an hotel after WWII. It is Grade II listed*

Morrab Gardens *derives its name from the Cornish for 'sea shore'. The Pidwell family built a house here in 1841. In the late 19thC the Penzance Corporation bought it for use as a public park with the house being rented out as the library*

Keep on this path for about 150m, passing the first gates out on the right and continuing until you reach the end of the gardens, beyond the fountain, where you will find an exit through large, wrought iron gates with the years 1889 – 1989 worked into their design. Beyond here the road goes slightly uphill with a modern office building on the right (make sure you've left the gardens at the right point!). You reach a junction with Victoria Place within 100m of the garden gates, notice the 1833 fountain on the left. Turn right here along Parade Street, passing a former Wesleyan chapel on the left, now a theatre, and the 18thC Phoenix House on the right, now restored after a serious fire in the 1990s.

Parade Street leads you back to Queen Street, turn right and repeat about 20m from earlier in the walk until you find Princes Street on the left. Go down here, enjoying an interesting juxtaposition of old and modern architecture. At the T-junction go left along New Street and this will lead you back to the Market House.

The final stage of the walk now goes left, passing the Market House on your right with a pillared shop opposite, once a bank. Beyond the market go right along Greenmarket and in about 50m turn right again along the pedestrianised shopping precinct with its attractive shop façias. The pedestrianised section continues for 250m, at its end turn right along Taroveor Road noticing the Bible Christian Sunday School from 1887 over on the left. Take the first right turning

Regent Square

down High Street, beside the Methodist Church which opened as a Bible Christian Chapel in 1879. Interestingly, High Street is a residential road rather than a shopping area.

> **Devon and Cornwall Bank:** *The Victorian, granite-pillared building which currently houses a health food shop was originally built for the Devon and Cornwall Bank in 1889. The bank was established c. 1832 and had 55 branches throughout Devon, Cornwall and Dorset by the time it was absorbed into Lloyds Bank in 1906*

Go down High Street with a lovely view of the dome atop the Market House. The road narrows and you reach a T-junction at which you go left along Bread Street, passing Old Brewery Yard on the left. In 100m you reach The Arcade on the right with steps leading back down to Market Jew Street. Descend these, turning right at the bottom to once more reach the Market House and the point from which you started.

Morrab Gardens

Walk 14
Fowey
Distance: 1.8 miles / 2.9km

Fowey is one of the loveliest of Cornwall's coastal towns and harbours, steeped in history and tales of piracy. The enticing, narrow ways are redolent of an earlier, romantic age enhanced by the strong association with Daphne du Maurier whose festival takes place here annually. Fowey's seaside cliff location means that there are a few ascents and descents in this walk but it is on paved paths throughout. It offers lovely views, delightful cottages and a good selection of tea shop stops.

Start point: Old Station Yard Car Park, Passage Lane, PL23 1JS

Directions to start: Fowey is situated at the mouth of the River Fowey in south Cornwall. It can be accessed off the A390 via the A3082 at St. Blazey or the B3269 near Lostwithiel

Parking: Old Station Yard Car Park, Passage Lane

Public transport: Fowey is served by buses from: St. Austell, Liskeard, Plymouth, Lostwithiel, Truro, Par, St. Blazey etc. Bus operators include First in Devon & Cornwall, Roselyn Coaches and Western Greyhound. Timetables available online at www.travelinesw.com. Nearest railway stations are Par (3.2 miles) and Lostwithiel (5 miles)

Refreshments: The Lifebuoy Café, 8 Lostwithiel St, 07715 075869; Pinky Murphy's Café, 19 North St, 01726 832512

Toilets: Caffa Mill Car Park and Town Quay

Nearby places to stay: Artist's House, 40 Vicarage Meadow, 01726 833680; The Dwelling House, 6 Fore St, 01726 833662; Upton House, 2 Esplanade, 01726 832732

Places of interest: Daphne du Maurier Literary Centre, 5 South St, 01726 833616; Fowey Museum, Trafalgar Square, 01726 833513

Market days: None

Authors' tip: If time allows we recommend a short trek to the south of town to visit Readymoney Cove. St. Catherine's Castle, which overlooks this small sandy cove, can be reached on foot via the coast path. Celebrated author Daphne du Maurier rented the nearby Readymoney Cottage in 1942/3. There is an annual festival dedicated to her which takes place in Fowey each May

Walk out of the car park and turn left down Passage Lane. The road becomes Station Road, the library is to your left and you pass Caffa Mill Car Park, which was rather more pricey than the one we parked in. Keep ahead through this

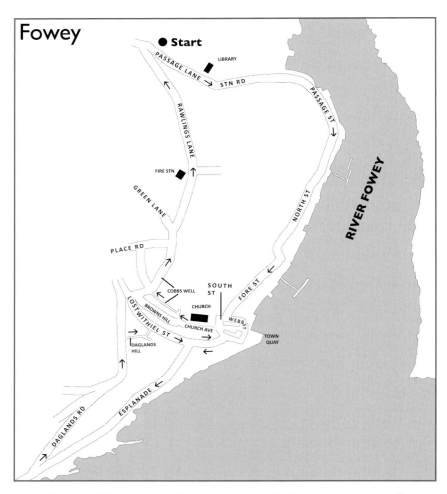

area of lovely old cottages and town houses with, from time to time, glimpses of the Fowey Estuary to your left and Polruan across the water.

Pass Passage Slip on your left and keep ahead on Passage Street. These delightful, narrow roads feel very ancient and appealing but please bear in mind that you share them with cars. Pass the late 19thC former Wesleyan Church on the right, the road is now North Street, and beyond here bends left then right to become Fore Street. The steps ahead at this bend are Bull Hill, an enticing backwater but not part of the route – explore if you wish. Continue down Fore Street. Even to someone who isn't fond of shopping this is an appealing place, full of interesting independent shops. Savour this area with its venerable buildings until you reach a T-junction. Here the walk turns right towards the church but first go left along Webb Street if you wish to visit the Town Quay. Back towards the church, turn left along South Street, first glancing up to the right where Bull Hill descends.

Fore Street: *This road has several very old buildings including the wonderful merchants' houses at number 27 and 29 with their timber-framed frontage. These are Grade II* listed and date from the early 17thC*

Pass the Church of St. Fimbarrus and Church Avenue on your right and follow the road as it then bends right up Lostwithiel Street. Pass The Old Telephone Exchange on the right and very soon you reach Varco's Corner, named for the grocer's shop which was once here. Turn left along The Esplanade.

Old Grammar School Garden: *Fowey Grammar School was situated in Daglands Road and closed in 1967. These gardens, known locally as 'The Quiet Gardens', were owned by the Grammar School's Trust Fund which still exists and which now rents the gardens to the town council for a peppercorn annual rent. All the plants in the garden are donated by local people*

Pass the Old Grammar School Garden on the left and the path down to the Fowey to Polruan Ferry. Keep on along The Esplanade and when Daglands Road

Bull Hill

comes in from the right turn sharp right up it and start to ascend as far as The Fowey Hotel. Pause here to regain breath and turn round to admire the view of St. Catherine's Castle on the headland behind you, above Readymoney Cove.

> **Readymoney Cove** *derives its name from the Cornish phrase 'roswyd basdowr' which has been corrupted to redeman and then readymoney and means a 'pebbly ford'. The building which now houses the toilet was once a limekiln, lime, sand and seaweed being brought up from the cove to fertilise the fields inland. On one side of the cove is Neptune House. Daphne du Maurier stayed near here during WWII*

> **St. Catherine's Castle** *has seen centuries of active service. It stands on the headland above Readymoney Cove and was constructed in 1536 during the reign of Henry VIII to repel Spanish marauders. Its construction was supervised by the Treffry family of Place House. During the mid 19thC it was restored and a gun battery was constructed below it for defence during the Crimean war. It was also modified for use as a battery and lookout point during WWII*

When you've had a breather continue up Daglands Road. A higher road comes to join you from the left, keep ahead enjoying occasional river views to the right until you find a tarmac footpath on the right between numbers 11 and 15. This

Town Quay

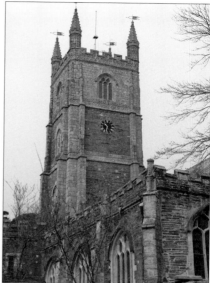

Fore Street   *St. Fimbarrus' Church*

is Daglands Hill. Go down here, knees in gear, and within about 50m you find some steps going left. Descend these, glancing up to admire the striking roofscape of the Grade I listed Place House. Place has been the private home of the Treffry family since the 13thC. It isn't open to the public. You will also have a good view of the church tower as you go down.

At the bottom of the steps walk ahead to the road. This is Lostwithiel Street again, turn right downhill passing more quaint cottages. You return to Varco's Corner, retrace your steps round to the left towards the parish church, noting the Fowey Museum opposite on Trafalgar Square. When you reach the church, go in. It's well-worthy of a visit, as is the Museum.

Fowey Museum *is housed in a venerable Grade II* listed building dating back to the 15thC. It may once have been a merchant house but was subsequently used as the Town Hall*

Fowey Church *is dedicated to St. Fimbarrus or Finn Barr, Bishop of Cork in the 7thC who stayed in Fowey whilst on pilgrimage to Rome and built a small church, replacing an even older one dedicated to St. Goran. A Norman church was built here in 1150 but the font is now all that remains of that 12thC*

The Rashleigh Almshouses

St. Fimbarrus' Church

church. The building was subsequently destroyed, possibly by pirates who were a very active species in Cornwall, and was reconstructed in the early 14thC. It was then damaged by the French in the mid 15thC and again rebuilt. Successive restorations have resulted in a very fine, Grade I listed church. Stand by the font under the bell tower and look down the nave towards the east window then walk the length of the church to get the view in the other direction and to fully admire the high, elegant lines of the arched bell tower

Leave the church and turn right out of the porch along the path, ascending steps to bear left up to Church Avenue. Turn right and follow the church railings round behind the church, but first glance left up the attractive-looking Browns Hill on the far side of this area. The railings lead towards a gate into the environs of Place House and just before this you see another lane ascending left. Go up here, this is Cobbs Well. Pass the Rashleigh Almshouses then ascend steps.

Rashleigh Almshouses *were built in 1625 by this wealthy merchant family for 'eight poor widows' and an allowance was made for the women to live on*

At the top of the steps turn right along a high-walled lane with a railing up the middle. This leads to a junction with Place Road on the left, keep ahead, passing Green Lane on the left as the road you are on bends right. This is Rawlings Lane. Follow it through a more modern-day Fowey, passing a cul-de-sac on the right and soon leaving the town behind. The road drops through a nice wooded area – keep to the pavement on the left hand side. At the T-junction turn right and you will find the car park from which you started on the left.

Helston
Distance: 1¼ miles / 2km

Helston is known all over the world for its annual celebration of spring, the 'furry' or 'Flora' dance. This dates from pre-Christian times and takes place in early May every year – a good time to visit. This lovely town has some fascinating history to be found along this short walk. There are a few ups and downs but the paths are mostly good. The approach to the church is on a slightly rough path but there is an option to avoid this.

Start point: Outside Helston Folk Museum, Market Place, TR13 8TH

Directions to start: Helston is located at the northern end of the Lizard Peninsula approximately 13 miles east of Penzance and 18 miles south west of Truro. It is accessible from the A394 which runs through the town

Parking: Wendron Street Car Park, Wendron St, TR13 8PS

Public transport: Helston is well served by buses from: Penzance, Falmouth, Truro, Redruth, Camborne etc. Bus operators are First in Devon & Cornwall, Travel Cornwall and Western Greyhound. Timetables available online at www.travelinesw.com. Nearest railway stations are Camborne (7½ miles) and Penryn (8½ miles)

Refreshments: The Blue Anchor Inn, 50 Coinagehall St, 01326 562821; Henlys Bar & Restaurant, 2 Church St, 01326 561141

Toilets: The Guildhall, Church St

Nearby places to stay: Hollow Tree House, 27 Church Hill, 01326 572410; Merther Uny Farm, Wendron, 01326 341459; Nansloe Manor, Meneage Rd, 01326 558400

Places of interest: Helston Folk Museum, Old Butter Market, Market Place, 01326 564027; National Seal Sanctuary, Gweek, 01326 221361; Poldark Mine, Wendron, 01326 573173; Roskilly's Ice cream and Organic Farm, Tregellast Barton, St. Keverne, 01326 280479

Market days: Country Market at The Guildhall every Friday, 7.45am–2pm. Farmers' Market at The Cattle Market Building, Boating Lake every 1st Saturday of the month, 9.30am–1.30pm

Authors' tip: Although a theme park primarily aimed at children consider a visit to Flambards, just south of town, for its Victorian Village alone. This wonderful recreation of the period with its 50+ shops set

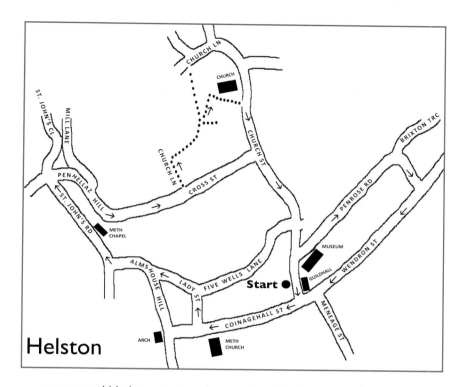

Helston

amongst cobbled streets is really worth a visit. Brown road signs guide you to Flambards (TR13 0QA)

Helston Folk Museum *was founded in 1949 and reflects all aspects of life of the people of Helston and the Lizard Peninsula. This mainly Victorian collection is displayed in the town's Market House, a construction originally designed in 1837 as two separate buildings – one for selling butter and eggs, the other for meat. Look out for the cannon at the front of the Museum. This was recovered from the wreck of the frigate HMS Anson which sank off Loe Bar in 1807 losing 100 sailors in the process*

The walk starts outside the Helston Folk Museum near the cannon which was taken from a shipwreck. Walk uphill from the cannon, along Church Street, and at the top turn right along Coinagehall Street with its little rivulet running alongside – you'll frequently see these in Helston. Although the Coinage Hall no longer exists its name remains and this is a broad road of delightful buildings – look out for the Old Carriage House on the right, the Angel Hotel on the left, the Methodist Church and the ancient Blue Anchor, amongst many others. You are walking towards a dominant arch at the bottom of the road.

__The Angel Hotel__ is a former coaching inn dating back to the mid 16thC when it was the town house of the Godolphin family, politicians and owners of local tin mines. It became an Inn in the late 17thC

__The Methodist Church__ was built in 1888 to replace a smaller chapel which became a Sunday School. The new building could take almost 1000 people

__The Blue Anchor,__ one of the oldest inns in the country which still has its own brewery, has been producing ale for 600 years. It started life as a monks' resting place, converting to a tavern at the Dissolution of the Monasteries. Spingo is the local brew

__The Monumental Arch__ contains 196 tons of granite. It was built in 1834 as a tribute to Humphry Millet Grylls, a local banker whose intervention saved the local tin mines and 1200 jobs. A popular man, he was just 45 when he died. His funeral procession was said to be 2 miles long. The arch's original railings were removed for scrap metal during WWII

Helston Museum

Just opposite The Blue Anchor turn right down Lady Street with its attractive cottages. Bend left with Lady Street and go to its end, then turn right to continue downhill. The road you are on (Almshouse Hill) bends left, keep along it until you reach a rather bendy T-junction. Turn right here, along St. John's Road, passing the Free Methodist Chapel on the right. Notice the inscription on the end gable stating 'St. John's Mission Hall 1920'.

You reach another T-junction opposite a cream-coloured cottage. Turn right uphill on Penhellaz Hill (there is nothing to tell you the name), proceeding with caution as there is no pavement. You pass a Freemasons' Hall on the right at Tubban. Look out for the inscription on the lintel dating this at 1916. Keep going uphill, there is a stone wall to your left surrounding the gardens of Penhellis House, a nursing home. The road becomes Cross Street with its elegant buildings. Just beyond Penhellis House look for tiny Church Lane on the left. This is the bit that can become slightly muddy further along, so if you don't wish to use this path go to the end of Cross Street and turn left to reach the church.

Those going left on Church Lane should follow it as it bends and soon you find steps up to the right leading into the churchyard. Explore this area, depending on the time of year the churchyard can be aptly floral, look out for the Henry Trengrouse monument. The church interior is beautiful.

The Blue Anchor, birthplace of Spingo

Church ceiling detail

*The spacious **St. Michael's Church** is Grade II* listed and was built in the mid 18thC to replace an earlier church which was burned down after a lightning strike. Funding was provided by the local aristocratic Godolphin family – there were then later additions to the building. Notice the intricate gilding on the chancel ceiling. From the gallery, looking along the length of the nave with its gracious plasterwork ceiling feels rather like looking into a Georgian ballroom*

*Cornwall has produced many renowned inventors and **Henry Trengrouse**, who was born, lived and is buried in Helston, was one of them. Distressed by the loss of life incurred at the sinking of HMS Anson he devised a rocket-propelled apparatus to get a line between wrecked ships and the shore in order to aid the hapless seafarers*

Leave the church from the main porch, bearing left down the path to the main gate out of the churchyard. Go down the steps to Church Street, you pass Andrew Hall on the right.

***Andrew Hall** now a community hall, has accommodated legion children over the decades, first as the National School in 1828 and later as the Helston Voluntary Primary School. It was also used as a training venue by Bob Fitzsimmons. The building is Grade II listed*

Walk down Church Street, passing on the left the home of Helston Town Band and then The Willows. Pass Cross Street on the right (notice the pre-Norman Conquest preaching cross on the corner) and as Church Street bears right and starts to climb you pass Five Wells Lane on the right followed by Penrose Road on the left. Go left up Penrose Road with nice glimpses left across the rooftops to the church and on the right the grand edifice of the old Passmore Edwards

Church interior

School from 1897 (see note in Truro Walk). At the time of writing this aspect of the building was boarded up and looking rather unloved. There are attractive cottages beyond here. The road bends right, go with it, and ahead of you at the T-junction you will see the thatched cottage where Bob Fitzsimmons was born. Turn right here, this is Wendron Street, and continue along passing the Godolphin Club on the right. You finish the walk at one of Helston's principal buildings: the 19thC, Grade II listed Guildhall. This is on your right with a footpath and steps adjacent, leading back down to your start point by the museum.

The Willows *another Grade II building, was built in 1776 as a private residence. It has some 20thC alterations and in 1939 it became council offices before reverting once more to residential use*

Preaching crosses *are to be found in many places throughout Cornwall and are probably survivors of the times when Celtic missionaries came to preach. They are thought to mark the spot where people gathered to listen*

Bob Fitzsimmons *was boxing's first world champion across three different weights. He was born in Helston in 1863, the youngest of 12 children, and emigrated to New Zealand with his family in the early 1870s. He married 4 times and died in America, of pneumonia, in 1917*

Bob Fitzsimmons early home

Church Street

Town Walks in Devon

by

Simone Stanbrook-Byrne and James Clancy

Town Walks in Devon is a collection of 15 circular walks which take you on journeys of exploration around some of Devon's most beautiful towns. You will discover hidden backwaters and well-kept secrets as well as finding the better-known landmarks.

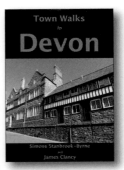

The walk directions are interspersed with notes on the history of the area and buildings en route, together with enticing photography, information on places to eat and stay and details of other places of interest nearby which are worthy of a visit, plus the market days for each town.

This book provides a wonderful glimpse into the towns of the county and will appeal to visitors and residents alike.

Towns Covered
Ashburton, Barnstaple, Brixham, Colyton, Dartmouth, Exeter, Great Torrington, Kingsbridge, Lynton & Lynmouth, Okehampton, Salcombe, Sidmouth, Tavistock, Tiverton, Totnes

Published: December 2011
Format: Paperback
Pages: 120pp
ISBN: 978-1-907942-05-1

Dimensions: 210x148mm
Publisher: Culm Valley Publishing

Price: £ 7.99

Orders can be placed at www.culmvalleypublishing.co.uk
or, alternatively, by telephone on 01884 849085

A Dozen Dramatic Walks in Cornwall

by

Simone Stanbrook-Byrne and James Clancy

Walkers are spoilt for choice in Cornwall. The aim of this book is to take you to the most spectacular scenery the county has to offer. Magnificent coastline and wild moorland contrast with delightful villages and pockets of verdant woodland.

A Dozen Dramatic Walks in Cornwall guides you on 12 outstanding circular routes.

Stunning photography and clear route instructions, together with details of local refreshment stops, places to stay and nearby places of interest, are all designed to make for the ultimate day out.

History notes, authors' tips and pointers on natural history are also included.

The *Dozen Dramatic Walks* series finds great favour with photographers who discover plenty of subject matter along these superb routes.

The Walks
1 Trebarwith Strand & Tintagel 2 Bodinnick & the Fowey estuary 3 St. Anthony Head 4 Lizard & Kynance Cove 5 Helford River & Frenchman's Creek 6 Polzeath, 7 Treen & Porthcurno 8 Zennor 9 Talland Bay & Polperro 10 Bodmin Moor & the Cheesewring 11 Boscastle & Rocky Valley 12 Chapel Porth, St. Agnes Head & Trevaunance Cove

Published: July 2011
Format: Paperback
Pages: 88pp
ISBN: 978-1-907942-03-7

Dimensions: 210x148mm
Publisher: Culm Valley Publishing

Price: £ 5.99

Orders can be placed at www.culmvalleypublishing.co.uk
or, alternatively, by telephone on 01884 849085

A Dozen Dramatic Walks in Devon

by

Simone Stanbrook-Byrne and James Clancy

These 12 circular routes, which incorporate some of Devon's most stunning scenery, are for walkers who like drama, amazing views and a sense of accomplishment at the end of the day.

Taking in some of Devon's most beautiful landscapes, this guide is primarily aimed at those who don't mind putting a little effort into their day's walking. However, options on shorter or easier routes are given where practical for those who prefer less of a challenge.

Encompassing the best of what Devon has to offer, the clearly-described routes introduce walkers to glorious coastline, expansive moorland and deep gorges, as well as gentle, picturesque river valleys and idyllic villages.

More than just a walking guide, *A Dozen Dramatic Walks in Devon* includes details of local watering holes for refreshment, places to stay and nearby places of interest. Historic notes, authors' tips and pointers on natural history are also included.

The exceptional photography which accompanies each walk tempts the reader to venture out and share the authors' love of Devon's great outdoors.

The Walks

1 Drewsteignton & the Teign Gorge 2 Noss Mayo & The Warren 3 Little Switzerland 4 Meldon & the High Tors 5 Trentishoe & the Heddon Valley 6 North Devon's Glorious Beaches 7 Exotic East Portlemouth 8 The Doone Valley 9 Bolt Head & Soar Mill Cove 10 Bigbury-on-Sea & Burgh Island 11 Tavy Cleave 12 Branscombe & the Hooken Undercliff

Published: January 2011   **Dimensions**: 210x148mm
Format: Paperback   **Publisher**: Culm Valley Publishing
Pages: 88pp
ISBN: 978-1-907942-00-6   **Price**: £ 5.99

Orders can be placed at www.culmvalleypublishing.co.uk or, alternatively, by telephone on 01884 849085

A Dozen Dramatic Walks in Dorset

by
Simone Stanbrook-Byrne and James Clancy

This fourth book in the *Dozen Dramatic* series provides twelve circular walks through some of Dorset's most dramatic scenery.

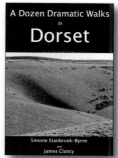

The book introduces the walker to some of the best areas of the county: lovely coastline, historic hillforts, tucked away footpaths and idyllic villages.

Taking in Dorset's beautiful landscapes, the guide is aimed at those who seek thirst-quenching views and a good day out in the open air. The 'drama' is in the scenery so the walking isn't necessarily strenuous. As with all CVP books, the routes are clearly and accurately described.

Each route includes details of refreshment stops, places to stay and nearby places of interest. Historic notes, authors' tips and pointers on natural history are also included.

Illustrated throughout, the book tempts both visitor and resident to explore Dorset's great outdoors.

The Walks
1 Studland Bay 2 Worth Matravers 3 Lulworth Cove 4 Portlesham 5 Burton Bradstock 6 Seatown and Golden Cap 7 Powerstock and Eggardon Hill 8 Pilsdon Pen 9 Cerne Abbas and Buckland Newton 10 Plush 11 Child Okeford 12 Melbury Abbas.

Published: July 2012
Format: Paperback
Pages: 88pp
ISBN: 978-1-907942-04-4

Dimensions: 210x148mm
Publisher: Culm Valley Publishing

Price: £ 5.99

Orders can be placed at www.culmvalleypublishing.co.uk
or, alternatively, by telephone on 01884 849085

Stannary Palace, Lostwithiel

Mallards, Trenance Gardens, Newquay

All images used in this book are available as cards and prints from Culm Valley Publishing
www.culmvalleypublishing.co.uk